Study Guide

for

Exceptional Learners
Introduction to Special Education
Eighth Edition

Study Guide

for

Hallahan and Kauffman
Exceptional Learners
Introduction to Special Education
Eighth Edition

Prepared by

E. Paula Crowley
Illinois State University

Allyn and Bacon
Boston   London   Toronto   Sydney   Tokyo   Singapore

ISBN 0-205-29820-6

Printed in the United States of America

10 9 8 7 6 5 4 3 2   04 03 02 01 00 99

Table of Contents

Preface

This Study Guide is designed to accompany *Exceptional Learners: Introduction to Special Education* (8th ed.) by Daniel P. Hallahan and James M. Kauffman. This Guide follows the chapter sequence of your text. It brings critical points to your attention and it offers you sample questions which will guide your preparation for examinations. Furthermore, it offers you exercises which require you to think independently, synthesize your knowledge, and analyze your growing understanding of the field.

This Study Guide is a guidebook in the classical sense. Guidebooks are designed to show travelers the way through an unfamiliar and even remote terrain. This Guide is designed to show you the way as you journey through countless new facts, concepts, and ideas. It is intended to focus your study, organize your ideas, and give you multiple opportunities to use your knowledge in question after question. This guide is meant only as a guide, and it should not limit your independent pursuit of specific areas of particular interest to you. For example, your textbook contains numerous references throughout, and these provide you with additional resources to further enrich and extend your studies of the field of special education.

Using This Study Guide

This Study Guide contains thirteen chapters. Each chapter contains five subsections which are designed to serve several purposes. First, each chapter provides you with a guide to important points to remember and ideas to evaluate in each area of exceptionality. Second, new vocabulary, concepts, and ideas are selected from each chapter of your textbook and listed along with their page numbers. You are asked to define each term. Following this, numerous questions and their answers are provided for each chapter. These are designed to assist you in your preparation for examinations. Finally, the enrichment activities are designed to enhance and extend your understanding of the field of special education.

In More Detail

As you begin your studies you will need your textbook, your class notes, your study guide, and a separate notebook on which you will write your ideas, insights, and your growing awareness of the field of special education.

The first section in each chapter of this Study Guide is designed to bring to your attention *Important Points to Remember* about each chapter. In your notebook you may wish to write any additional important points to remember.

The *Reflection and Discussion* sections bring specific provocative quotes from your textbook to your attention. These quotes are accompanied by their page numbers for quick reference back to your textbook. Following the quotes are questions, comments, as well as invitations for you to think about your own values and beliefs. The intent of this section is to provide you with a more in-depth understanding of the field of special education. You may wish to write your responses to the questions and comments from this section in your notebook.

The field of special education has its own history, heroes and heroines, milestones, vocabulary, and concepts. The *Define the Terms* sections bring critical terms to your attention accompanied by their page numbers. You may find it helpful to write the definitions of each term in your notebook.

At this point, you are ready for specific objective questions. The *Know the Content of This Chapter* sections contain five types of commonly used questions which you will often find on examinations. These include *Matching*, *True or False*, *Fill in the Blank*, *Multiple Choice*, and *Short Answer*. Following each question is the page number which contains the answer to that question. In the event that you are unsure of a correct answer, the page number references to your textbook will be a helpful resource. The answers are provided for the matching, true or false, and multiple choice questions at the end of each chapter. In your notebook, you may wish to keep track of how well you are doing as you respond to each of these questions.

The *Enrichment* sections provide you with exercises which may greatly enhance your understanding of the field of special education. Some of these exercises involve reading novels related to specific disability areas or viewing films of particular interest. Other activities recommend that you have conversations with local special education teachers, school administrators, parents, and others in the field. In your notebook, you may want to write your answers to these questions, your thoughts on issues, and your responses to additional enrichment exercises you may develop which are of specific interest to you.

It is most important to keep in mind that this is a guide to your studies and in no way is it intended to limit you. Do not hesitate to go beyond it, seek out additional resources, and enter references and ideas in your notebook.

Finally, enjoy the unique journey you are about to begin!

Dedication

To Dan and Patrick

Acknowledgments

I would like to express my gratitude to Ray Short of Allyn and Bacon, who first approached me about writing this Study Guide. I fully appreciate the opportunity he gave me to assist students across the nation in becoming knowledgeable about the field of special education. Thanks to Karin Huang, Virginia Lanigan, and Diana Murphy of Allyn and Bacon, for their assistance to me during the development of this Guide. Thanks to Dan Hallahan and Jim Kauffman who reviewed a draft of this manuscript. I want to acknowledge their dedication which has for more than twenty years provided the field of special education with an excellent introductory text.

E.P.C.

Chapter 1

Exceptionality and Special Education

I. **Important Points to Remember**

*   The exact percentage of individuals who have disabilities in the United States is uncertain.

*   Several administrative plans are available for the education of exceptional children and youths.

*   Most school age students with disabilities receive their education primarily in general education classrooms.

*   Educational placements for students with disabilities range from a few special provisions made by teachers in general education classrooms to special self-contained classrooms in residential care facilities.

*   Special education means specially designed instruction that meets the unusual needs of exceptional students.

*   During the 1980s, the relationship between general and special education became a matter of great concern to policymakers, researchers and advocates for exceptional children.

*   Proposals for changing the relationship between general and special education came to be known as the Regular Education Initiative.

*   Many general educators participate in the education of students with disabilities.

*   Individuals with disabilities have been empowered by such legislation as IDEA in 1975 (then known as PL 94-142) anADA

1

*   Special educators are required to attain expertise in teaching students with unusual learning and behavioral problems.

II.   Reflection and Discussion

1.   "The study of exceptional learners is the study of *differences*. ... The study of exceptional learners is also the study of *similarities*" (p. 4). Do you agree with these statements? Why?

2.   "... we must not lose sight of the fact that the most important characteristics of exceptional learners are their abilities" (p. 6). Do you agree with this statement? State your rationale to support your perspective.

3.   "The concept of diversity is inherent in the definition of exceptionality; the need for special education is inherent in an educational definition" (p. 7). What do you think the authors mean by these statements? Do you agree or disagree with the authors? Defend your position with supporting rationale.

4.   "By federal law, an exceptional student is not to be identified as eligible for special education until careful assessment indicates that he/she is unable to make satisfactory progress in the regular school program without special services designed to meet his or her extraordinary needs" (p. 8). Write three underlying beliefs which are implied in this statement.

5.   "There have always been exceptional learners, but there have not always been special educational services to address their needs" (p. 24). Describe three salient implications of this statement.

6.   "In the prerevolutionary era, the most society had offered children with disabilities was protection--asylum from a cruel world into which they did not fit and in which they could not survive with dignity, if they could survive at all" (p. 24). Compare and contrast this statement with what modern society offers children with disabilities.

2

7. "… And many (perhaps most) of today's vital, controversial issues have been issues ever since the dawn of special education" (p. 24). Describe at least three such issues and provide a rationale for why they remain issues today.

8. "The primary intent of the special education laws passed during the past two decades has been to require educators to focus on the needs of individual students with disabilities" (p. 33). What, in your opinion, is the primary benefit of focusing on the needs of individual students? On what basis might this approach be criticized?

III. Define the Terms

Write a definition for each of the following terms.

1. disability (p. 6)

2. handicap (p. 6)

3. self-contained class (p. 14)

4. LRE (p. 15)

5. REI (p. 19)

6. IDEA (p. 28)

7. ADA (p. 28)

8. PL 94-142 (p. 28)

9. PL 99-457 (p. 28)

10. Hudson v. Rowley (p. 33)

11. IEP (p. 33)

12. IFSP (p. 38)

IV. Know the Content in this Chapter

A. Matching

a) LRE
b) REI
c) IDEA
d) ADA
e) PL 99-457
f) special day school
g) Hudson v. Rowley
h) IFSP
i) resource teacher

1. ___ provides individual or small-group instruction in the regular classroom or in another room in the school (p. 14).

2. ___ implies that a student should be separated from nondisabled classmates and from home, family and community as little as possible (p. 15).

3. ___ provides effective service for students with severe exceptionalities; special educators provide instruction in a segregated setting for the school day (p. 17).

4. ___ marked the 1980s with a radical call to merge special and general education (p. 19).

5. ___ ensures that all children and youths with disabilities have a right to a free appropriate public education (p. 28).

6. ___ mandates a free, appropriate public education for every child or youth between the ages of three and twenty-one regardless of the nature or severity of the disability he or she may have (p. 28).

7. ___ ensures the right of individuals with disabilities to equal opportunities in employment, transportation, public accommodations, state and local government, and telecommunications (p. 29).

8.   ___ ruled that appropriate education for a deaf child with a disability does not necessarily mean education that will produce the maximum possible achievement (p. 33).

9.   ___ requires assessment and statements of goals, needed services, and plans for implementation of services for infants and toddlers with disabilities (p. 38).

B.   True or False

1.   About one out of every ten children in the United States has a disability (p. 4). T or F

2.   At this point, special education professionals are able to identify the exact reason why a child has a specific disability (p. 4). T or F

3.   Special education means specially designed instruction that meets the unusual needs of an exceptional student (p. 12). T or F

4.   Over two-thirds of students with disabilities are educated primarily in regular classes with their age-appropriate peers (p. 15). T or F

5.   The least restrictive environment for one student with a disability may be highly restrictive for another student with a disability (p. 15). T or F

6.   Students who are considered at risk always have disabilities (p. 19). T or F

7.   Most of the originators of special education were American physicians (p. 25). T or F

8.   PL 99-457 was the first public law mandating free, appropriate public education for all children with disabilities (p. 28). T or F

9.   Federal, state, and local governments all share equally in the cost of funding special education programs (p. 28). T or F

10.   There is a standard IEP format used in all schools (p. 34). T or F

11.	The IFSP requires family involvement, coordination of services, and plans for making the transition into preschool (p. 38). T or F

12.	Parents of children with disabilities are powerless in the face of school administrators who do not want to provide appropriate education and related services for learners with disabilities (p. 39).

**C.	Fill in the Blank**

1.	A _____ is an inability to do something, a diminished capacity to perform in a specific way (p. 6).

2.	John can no longer run due to the progress of his muscular dystrophy; he now has a _____ (pp. 6, 7).

3.	Government figures show that about _____ percent of students in the United States receive special education (p. 12).

4.	_____ is designed to provide instruction that meets the educational needs of exceptional learners (pp. 12-13).

5.	Hospital and homebound instruction is most often required by students who have _____ disabilities (p. 14).

6.	For Susan, who has a physical disability, the _____ is the general education classroom. However, the committee agreed that due to John's severe behavior disorder, he is most appropriately placed in a self-contained classroom (p. 15).

7.	The three most common placements where students with disabilities receive their education are _____, _____, _____ (pp. 15-16).

8.	The historical roots of special education are found primarily in the early _____ (p. 24).

9.	An example of a professional organization devoted to special education is _____ (p. 27).

10.	_____ was the first federal law mandating free, appropriate public education for all children with disabilities (p. 28).

11. The building is not accessible to individuals with physical disabilities. This is a violation of _____ (p. 28).

12. _____ mandated an Individualized Family Service Plan (IFSP) for infants and toddlers with disabilities (p. 38).

D.   Multiple Choice

1.   Which of the following factors does not contribute to the difficulty involved in determining the number of children and youths with exceptionalities? (pp. 11-12).
    a)   vagueness in definitions
    b)   frequent changes in entry and exit numbers of students to and from special education programs
    c)   the role of schools in determining exceptionality
    d)   frequent changes in definitions

2.   What percentage of students of school age receive special education services in the late 1990s? (p. 12).
    a)   15 percent   d)   5 percent
    b)   7 percent   e)   10 percent
    c)   8 percent

3.   In which disability areas is there the largest increase in the numbers of identified students over the past 20 years? (p. 12).
    a)   other health impairments and physical disabilities
    b)   mental retardation and learning disabilities
    c)   speech and language disorders
    d)   learning disabilities and emotional and behavioral disorders
    e)   deafness and blindness

4.   Hallahan and Kauffman state that the most important goal of special education is: (p. 13)
    a)   to provide appropriate instructional materials for exceptional learners
    b)   to instruct exceptional learners using appropriate methodology
    c)   to capitalize on the abilities of exceptional learners
    d)   to make education available to all students
    e)   none of the above

5. The most integrated placement for students with disabilities is: (pp. 13-14)
   a) the regular classroom
   b) a resource classroom
   c) a special class
   d) a residential school
   e) none of the above

6. The least restrictive environment for students with learning disabilities is: (p. 18)
   a) resource rooms
   b) general education classrooms
   c) self-contained classrooms
   d) the child's home
   e) none of the above

7. Special educators must attain special expertise in all of the following except: (pp. 22-24)
   a) academic instruction of students with learning problems
   b) management of serious behavior problems
   c) early intervention programming
   d) the use of technological advances
   e) knowledge of special education law

8. During the closing years of the 18th century effective procedures were devised for teaching students with: (p. 24)
   a) mental retardation
   b) emotional and behavioral disorders
   c) blindness and deafness
   d) learning disabilities
   e) physical disabilities

9. Most of the originators of special education were in the field(s) of: (p. 26)
   a) medicine
   b) psychology and psychiatry
   c) education
   d) sociology
   e) all of the above

10. To whom are the beginnings of special education attributed? (p. 25).
   a) Seguin
   b) Pinel
   c) Itard
   d) Gallaudet
   e) Howe

11. Samuel Gridley Howe made a unique contribution to the field of special education in the areas of: (pp. 25-26)
    a) deafness, blindness and mental retardation
    b) mental retardation and physical disabilities
    c) social consciousness raising and blindness
    d) development of educational methods and deafness
    e) none of the above

12. Parents' organizations typically do *not* serve which one of the following functions? (p. 27).
    a) providing the structure for obtaining needed services for children
    b) securing the financial support which is essential for the provision of special education services
    c) providing information regarding services and potential resources
    d) providing an informal group for parents who understand one another's problems and needs and help one another deal with anxieties and frustrations
    e) none of the above

13. When was the Individuals with Disabilities Education Act passed? (p. 28).
    a) 1991
    b) 1975
    c) 1990
    d) 1992
    e) 1985

14. Which law was passed in 1990 and ensures the rights of individuals with disabilities to nondiscriminatory treatment in areas of employment, transportation, public accommodations, state, and local government and telecommunications? (p. 28).
    a) IDEA
    b) ADA
    c) PL 94-142
    d) PL 99-457
    e) PL 101-476

15. When an IEP is prepared as intended by the mandates of IDEA, all the following have been met except: (p. 34)
    a) the student's needs have been carefully assessed
    b) goals and objectives are clearly stated so that progress in reaching them can be evaluated
    c) the precise teaching materials to be used are outlined in explicit language
    d) a team of professionals and the parents/guardians have worked together to design an education program which best meets the student's needs

E. Short Answer

1. Differentiate between the terms disability and handicap and provide an example to support your analysis (p. 6).

2. Describe the factors which contribute to the difficulty in establishing definitive and precise counts of how many individuals have disabilities in the United States (pp. 10-12).

3. What two factors determine who educates exceptional students and where they receive their education? (p. 13).

4. What is the purpose of selecting the least restrictive environment for a student? Provide an example of two students for whom the same setting is not the least restrictive environment (pp. 12-18).

5. Children under the age of six more commonly receive their education in separate schools and in separate programs. Why? (pp. 17-18).

6. Before referring a child for an evaluation, what three actions must be taken? (p. 21).

7. Do you accept or reject the hypotheses that a large number of students in public schools not identified as disabled or gifted share many of the characteristics of those who are exceptional? Why? (pp. 20-22).

8. Do you believe that all educators should participate in the education of students with disabilities? Why or why not? Defend your position with convincing rationale (pp. 20-24).

9. In what ways do the professional obligations of general and special educators differ? (pp. 20-24).

10. The field of special education developed in association with other disciplines. What simultaneously developing disciplines contributed to the development of special education? (pp. 24-27).

11. The ideas of Itard and Seguin formed the foundation for present-day special education. Explain five of these ideas to a peer (pp. 25-26).

12. What is the major intent of the Americans with Disabilities Act? (p. 28).

13. What is the major intent of the special education laws passed during the last two decades? (pp. 28-34).

14. What are the primary reasons which generally motivate special education litigation? (pp. 32-33).

15. What are the five components of IEPs which are central to legally correct and educationally useful plans? (p. 34).

16.   What are the primary criticisms of IEP critics? (pp. 33-37).

17.   What are the provisions of Individualized Family Service Plans?
        (pp. 38-39).

18.   Do you agree that special education has come a long way since it
        was introduced into American public education over a century ago?
        Why or why not? (p. 39).

V.   Enrichment Activities

1.   Make a list of the ways general educators participate in the
        education of students with disabilities. Write as many different
        ways as you can and compare your list with the set of expectations
        listed on pages 19-24 of this chapter.

2.   What are the gains and losses in having the Courts decide what
        IDEA means by "appropriate" education and "least restrictive
        environment"? What realistic alternatives might better serve the
        field today?

3.   Talk with a pioneer, an individual who has provided at least 20
        years of service in the field of special education, and ask him/her
        to describe how the field has changed over the years. What
        changes does this individual regard as positive? Are there
        changes in the field over the years which this individual regards as
        negative?

Answer Key for Chapter One

Matching		True or False		Multiple Choice	
1.	i	1.	T	1.	b
2.	a	2.	F	2.	e
3.	f	3.	T	3.	d
4.	b	4.	T	4.	c
5.	c	5.	T	5.	a
6.	e	6.	F	6.	b
7.	d	7.	F	7.	c
8.	g	8.	F	8.	c
9.	h	9.	F	9.	a
		10.	F	10.	c
		11.	T	11.	a
		12.	F	12.	b
				13.	c
				14.	b
				15.	c

Chapter 2

Current Trends and Issues

I. **Important Points to Remember**

*   Integration, early childhood programming, and programming for transition from secondary school to adulthood represent three current trends in the field of special education.

*   Participation of students with disabilities in general assessments of educational progress and discipline of students with disabilities represent additional current trends in the field of special education.

*   Today more individuals with disabilities are integrated into mainstream society than ever before.

*   The integration of individuals with disabilities into society is not a new concept; in fact, professionals have been advocating integration into mainstream society for more than 30 years.

*   The deinstitutionalization movement encouraged more and more individuals with disabilities to live with their families and integrate into their local communities.

*   Normalization suggests that both the means and the ends of education for individuals with disabilities should be as normal as possible.

*   Though many special educators and nonspecial education professionals argue for full inclusion of individuals with disabilities, the notion of full inclusion has met with considerable resistance.

*   Advocates for individuals with disabilities suggest that we must use labels with much sensitivity to their negative connotation.

* Two cautions regarding the use of labels--use person first language and use labels only to enhance clear communication about individuals with disabilities.
* Some individuals with disabilities participate in the disability rights movement.

* Disability rights activists have been active on a variety of fronts including lobbying legislators and employers and criticizing the media for biased and stereotypical coverage of individuals with disabilities.

* Professionals in special education and related areas increasingly emphasize the importance of early intervention for young children with disabilities.

* Positive postschool outcomes for students with disabilities remain a concern for many special education professionals.

II. Reflection and Discussion

1. "The trend of integrating people with disabilities into the larger society began in the 1960s and continues stronger than ever today" (p. 44). Do you support the idea of integrating individuals with disabilities into the larger society? Why or why not?

2. "Even though the originators of the normalization principle saw the need for a variety of service delivery options--including residential institutions, special schools, and special classes--more recently, some have interpreted normalization to mean the abolishment of such separate settings" (p. 46). Do you believe that separate settings have an important role in the field of special education or do you believe that they should all be eliminated? Explain your rationale.

3. "For the most part, special educators have been proud of this continuum of placements. They have viewed the LRE concept as the lifeblood of special education ..." (p. 48). Do you believe that the provision of a continuum of placements and LRE are noble accomplishments of special education professionals? Present a brief rationale to support your answer.

4. "Some people fear that a 'special education' label can cause a child to feel unworthy or to be viewed by the rest of society as a deviant, hence grow to feel unworthy" (p. 49). What alternatives are available for those who believe that "special education" labels have negative connotations for individuals with disabilities?

5. "... proponents (of full inclusion) tend to approach issues of integration from an ethical rather than an empirical perspective" (p. 57). What are the dangers of a disregard for the data over arguments based solely on ethical charges of inequality?

6. "The notion of full inclusion has met with considerable resistance" (p. 58). Are you surprised by this? Why or why not?

7. "Children whose disabilities are diagnosed at a very young age ... have severe and multiple disabilities" (p. 69). Why do children who are diagnosed at a young age tend to have severe and multiple disabilities?

8. "We know that dropout and employment rates are far too high for all youths ... but the outlook for students with disabilities may be even worse" (p. 73). What factors explain the high dropout rates and the poor outlook for students with disabilities?

III. Define the Terms

Write a definition for each of the following terms.

1. normalization (p. 44)

2. deinstitutionalization (p. 47)

3. full inclusion (p. 48)

4. LRE (p. 48)

5. labeling (p. 49)

6.   pull-out programs (p. 51)

7.   disability rights movement (p. 52)
8.   handicapism (p. 52)

9.   prereferral teams (p. 61)

10.   collaborative consultation (p. 62)

11.   cooperative teaching (pp. 62-64)

12.   cooperative learning (pp. 64-65)

13.   peer tutoring (pp. 64-65)

14.   partial participation (p. 65)

15.   "standards-based" reforms (p. 66)

16.   curriculum materials designed to change attitudes (p. 64)

17.   Kids on the Block (p. 64)

18.   developmental delay (p. 69)

19.   supported employment (pp. 74-76)

20.   job coach (pp. 75-76)

21.   Goals 2000 (pp. 77)

22.   zero tolerance (p. 79)

23.   mandatory sentencing (p. 79)

24.   manifestation determination (p. 80)

IV.   Know the Content in This Chapter

A.   Matching

a) labeling
b) normalization
c) continuum of alternative placements
d) collaborative consultation
e) prereferral teams
f) the full-inclusion movement
g) deinstitutionalization
h) supported employment
i) developmental delay
j) disability rights movement
k) pull-out programs
l) cooperative teaching
m) Individualized Family Service Plan
n) mainstreaming
o) cooperative learning
p) peer tutoring
q) partial participation
r) curriculum materials designed to change attitudes
s) handicapism
t) job coach

1. ____ is the philosophical belief that the means and the ends of education for students with disabilities should be as much like those for nondisabled students as possible (p. 44).

2. ____ caused more and more individuals with disabilities to move out of institutions and return to closer contact with their family homes and communities (p. 47).

3. ____ all students with disabilities attend all classes in their neighborhood schools and in the general education classroom (p. 48).

4. ____ assumes that there are alternatives along a continuum of restrictiveness, with residential institutions on one end and regular classes on the other (p. 48).

5. ____ causes some people to fear that children may feel unworthy or to be viewed by the rest of society as deviant and hence grow to feel unworthy (p. 49).

6. _____ permit students with disabilities to be removed from the general education classroom and to receive their instruction in a more specialized setting (p. 51).

7. _____ these activists believe that individuals with disabilities are an oppressed minority (p. 52).

8. _____ is a set of assumptions and practices which cause individuals with disabilities to be treated differently and unequally (p. 52).

9. _____ work with general education teachers to recommend different strategies for working with children exhibiting academic and/or behavioral problems (pp. 61-62).

10. _____ is the practice of placing students with disabilities in general education classrooms with their nondisabled peers for all or only a few subjects (p. 61).

11. _____ the process in which the special educator and the general educator assume equal responsibility for students with disabilities and neither one assumes more authority in making recommendations about how to teach the child (p. 62).

12. _____ general and special educators jointly teach in the same general education classroom composed of students with and without disabilities (pp. 62-64).

13. _____ may be organized so that students with disabilities work together with their nondisabled peers to solve problems or practice responses (p. 64).

14. _____ educational materials which enlighten nondisabled students about students with disabilities (p. 64).

15. _____ involves students with disabilities participating in general education classrooms at reduced levels (p. 65).

16. _____ involves one student in the role of tutor and the other in the role of tutee (pp. 64-65).

17. ___ a term used to encompass a variety of disabilities of infants and young children indicating that they are significantly behind the norm for development in one or more areas (p. 69).

18. ___ is a plan which focuses on the needs of the family as well as the needs of the child (pp. 69-70).

19. ___ provides on-site training that is gradually reduced as the worker is able to function on the job more independently (pp. 75-76).

20. ___ a method of integrating people with disabilities, who cannot work independently, into competitive employment (p. 74).

B. True or False

1. Special education professionals agree about how and where to integrate students with disabilities (p. 44). T or F

2. Some individuals who are deaf prefer to associate with people who are deaf, and for them, normalization does not mean integration with the larger society (p. 46). T or F

3. The idea of integrating students with disabilities is hardly new. Efforts to integrate students with disabilities have been going on for more than 30 years (pp. 46-47). T or F

4. All large institutions for individuals with mental retardation are dehumanizing (p. 47). T or F

5. Educational programming for students with disabilities has historically been built on the assumption that a variety of service delivery options need to be available (p. 48). T or F

6. Research data on the effects of labeling has been inconclusive (pp. 49-50). T or F

7. For the most part parents, teachers, and students are satisfied with the degree of integration into general education now experienced by students with disabilities (p. 58). T or F

8. Most special educators are in favor of some degree of mainstreaming (p. 61). T or F

9. There is precise agreement on who should serve on prereferral teams (p. 61). T or F

10. Children whose disabilities are diagnosed at a very young age tend to be those with specific syndromes (p. 69). T or F

11. In recent years professionals in the area of early intervention have advocated for home-based programs for young children with disabilities (p. 70). T or F

12. Published figures on dropout rates must be viewed with caution because there are so many different ways of defining dropout and of computing statistics (p. 73). T or F

C. Fill in the Blank

1. A key principle behind the trend towards the integration of people with disabilities into society is called _____ (p. 44).

2. The two movements which have helped to speed up the integration of individuals with disabilities are _____ and _____ (p. 47).

3. _____ try to keep referrals to special education down by stressing that general educators try as many alternative strategies as possible before deciding that difficult-to-teach students need to become the primary responsibility of special educators (p. 61).

4. When involved in _____, general and special educators work together stressing mutuality and reciprocity (p. 62).

5. When students with and without disabilities work together in a structured cooperative manner they are engaged in _____ (p. 64).

6.   An example of curricula designed to develop more positive attitudes toward students with disabilities is _____ (p. 64).

7.   When students with disabilities participate, on a reduced basis, in virtually all activities in the general education classroom, they are engaged in _____ (p. 65).

8.   Access to the general education curriculum is emphasized by individuals involved in the _____ movement (p. 66).

9.   _____ is designed to meet the educational needs of very young children with disabilities (pp. 68-69).

10.   An _____ is similar to an individualized education plan but has a broader focus which includes the child and the family (pp. 68-70).

11.   The term _____ has been coined to describe a new set of disabilities (p. 73).

12.   _____ is designed to assist persons with disabilities who cannot function independently in competitive employment (pp. 74-76).

13.   A _____ provides on-site training to individuals with disabilities. The training is gradually reduced as the worker is able to function more independently (pp. 75-76).

14.   _____ is a procedure in which school officials determine whether a student's behavior is or is not a manifestation of his or her disability (p. 80).

D.   Multiple Choice

1.   Normalization is a philosophical belief supporting the idea that: (pp. 44-46)
     a)   individuals with disabilities should be viewed as normal by society

b) with little or no adjustment, individuals with disabilities may be educated along with their nondisabled peers

c) individuals with disabilities should live in and be educated in an environment that is as normal as possible, maintaining personal behaviors and characteristics which are as normative as possible

d) following integration and over a long period of time, individuals with disabilities begin to take on the characteristics of the larger population

2. The deinstitutionalization movement began because: (pp. 46-47)
   a) care in institutions became too expensive
   b) institutions were largely populated by individuals who were deaf and blind
   c) in the 1960s and 1970s prevailing beliefs supported the idea that individuals with disabilities should live close to their families and in their own local communities
   d) a and b only
   e) none of the above

3. Most definitions of inclusion contain which three of the following elements? (p. 48).
   a) general educators, not special educators assume primary responsibility for students with disabilities
   b) all students with disabilities attend their neighborhood schools
   c) students with disabilities receive their education from general educators who are willing to teach them
   d) all students with disabilities, no matter the type or severity of disability, attend all classes in general education, i.e. no separate special education classes
   e) a, b, and d only

4. Which of the following is seen as a problem in labeling children with disabilities? (pp. 49-50).
   a) Labels can affect self-esteem.
   b) Children can develop feelings of unworthiness due to the labels assigned to them.
   c) Labels can cause individuals with disabilities to be viewed negatively.
   d) All of the above are true.

5. Some professionals argue that labeling is necessary because: (pp. 49-50)
    a) individuals with special problems are different
    b) labels are merely words we use to communicate
    c) labels spotlight the unique needs of individuals with disabilities
    d) all of the above

6. Though some special educators have asserted that research shows pull-out programs to be ineffective, Hallahan and Kauffman and other critics of these data argue that: (pp. 51-52)
    a) research data on pull-out programs are methodologically flawed
    b) generally the researchers failed to randomly assign students to groups
    c) school personnel would be challenged for unethical professional behavior if they randomly assigned students to groups
    d) all of the above

7. Disability rights activists claim that: (p. 52)
    a) individuals with disabilities have a unique set of rights because of their disabilities
    b) children with disabilities must be educated in general education classrooms
    c) a separate Bill of Rights exists for individuals with disabilities
    d) individuals with disabilities are an oppressed minority

8. Which of the following basic strategies may be recommended for use by general and special educators when integrating students with disabilities? (p. 61).
    a) prereferral teams
    b) collaborative consultation
    c) cooperative teaching
    d) curriculum and instruction strategies

9. The major goal of prereferral teams is: (pp. 61-62)
    a) for parents and teachers to form teams before referring a child for special education services

b) for children and teachers to form a team before referral to special education

c) to encourage general educators to take responsibility for teaching students with special needs

d) none of the above

10. Which of the following statements is true? (p. 62).

a) In collaborative consultation, the special educator and the general educator assume equal responsibility for the education of students with disabilities.

b) When using collaborative consultation, neither the general educator nor the special educator assumes more authority for teaching students with disabilities.

c) Collaborative consultation can be used to keep difficult-to-teach students in the general education classroom.

d) All of the above are true.

11. Which of the following groups of students with disabilities do not work well in groups that demand cooperation? (p. 64).

a) students with visual and auditory disabilities

b) students who have learning disabilities

c) students with behavioral disorders and mental impairments

d) those who have communication disorders and physical disabilities

12. Partial participation refers to: (p. 65)

a) general education teachers partially participate in the education of children with disabilities

b) students with disabilities participate on a reduced basis in virtually all activities in the general education classroom

c) special educators participate only partially in the general education program

d) none of the above

13. Participation in general assessments of progress refers to: (p. 66)

a) students with disabilities involved in their own assessment

b) participating in assessments using the general assessment tools available in school settings

c) all students, those with and without disabilities will be held to higher standards of performance

d) none of the above

14. Hallahan and Kauffman view the many trends and issues in the field of special education as: (p. 81)
    a)   indicative of a field in chaos
    b)   a sign of health and vigor
    c)   exciting and challenging
    d)   b and c only
    e)   none of the above

E.   **Short Answer**

1.   What five major current trends described by Hallahan and Kauffman stand out in the field of special education? (p. 44).

2.   What two movements have helped to speed up integration efforts in recent years? (p. 46).

3.   Differentiate between full inclusion and a continuum of services (p. 48).

4.   What are the four premises of full inclusion as described by Hallahan and Kauffman? (pp. 48-49).

5.   Describe at least three advantages and three disadvantages of labeling (pp. 49-50).

6.   Individuals with disabilities are a heterogeneous population. What are the implications of this statement for viewing individuals with disabilities as a minority? (pp. 52-57).

7.   Do you support the idea that the consideration of individuals with disabilities as a minority group is a flawed concept? (p. 59).

8.   Provide three reasons to support the development of early intervention programs for children with disabilities (pp. 68-69).

9. Write seven reasons why the number of children with disabilities is increasing in the United States (pp. 72-73).

10. Explain what professionals in special education and related areas mean when they refer to "a new morbidity" (p. 73).

11. Describe three quality of life domains which are relevant to transition planning (p. 74).

12. Why is discipline of students with disabilities a complex issue? (pp. 78-81).

V.   Enrichment Activities

1. Analyze the availability of the "Kids on the Block" puppet show in your local area. Attend a session of this show and conduct an informal study of its effectiveness in changing the audience's attitudes toward children with disabilities.

2. Read *Christmas in Purgatory: A Photographic Essay on Mental Retardation* by B. Blatt and F. Kaplan (Allyn & Bacon, 1966). Consider why this text was a significant contribution in the development of the field of special education. In your opinion what issue would a similar consciousness--raising text address in today's society?

3. Write an essay to persuade an audience that individuals with disabilities either are or are not integrated into mainstream society today. Provide specific examples to support your arguments.

4. Read *Ghosts from the Nursery: Tracing the Roots of Violence* by R. Karr-Morse and M. S. Wiley (Atlantic Monthly Press, 1997). What are the implications of this book for early childhood programming? What are its implications for violence prevention?

Answer Key for Chapter Two

Matching		True or False		Multiple Choice	
1.	b	1.	F	1.	c
2.	g	2.	T	2.	c
3.	f	3.	T	3.	e
4.	c	4.	F	4.	d
5.	a	5.	T	5.	d
6.	k	6.	T	6.	d
7.	j	7.	T	7.	d
8.	s	8.	T	8.	d
9.	e	9.	F	9.	c
10.	n	10.	T	10.	a
11.	d	11.	T	11.	c
12.	l	12.	T	12.	b
13.	o			13.	d
14.	r			14.	d
15.	q				
16.	p				
17.	i				
18.	m				
19.	t				
20.	h				

Chapter 3

Multicultural and Bilingual Aspects of Special Education

I.   **Important Points to Remember**

*   The purpose of multicultural education is to change educational institutions and curricula so that they will provide equal educational opportunities to students regardless of their gender, social class, ethnic group, race, disability, or cultural identity.

*   Educators are becoming increasingly aware of the extent to which differences among cultural and ethnic groups affect children's schooling.

*   Educators must guard against stereotypes which might lead to the belief that students' cultural identity is sufficient to explain their academic achievement and/or economic success.

*   Teachers must plan experiences that teach about culture and provide models of cultural awareness and acceptance and the appreciation of cultural diversity.

*   Accepting and fostering cultural diversity may be done while students learn the skills they need to survive and prosper in the larger context of American macroculture.

II.   **Reflection and Discussion**

1.   "Education that takes full advantage of the cultural diversity in our schools and the larger world requires much critical analysis and planning" (p. 88). Do you agree or disagree with the idea of taking full advantage of our cultural diversity? Defend your position with a convincing rationale.

2. "People with certain exceptionalities can develop their own microcultures" (p. 100). Provide an example to illustrate your understanding of this concept.

3. "Should a student who speaks no English be forced to give up his or her native language in school and to learn to use only English (ignoring the cultural-linguistic differences)?" (p. 104). What do you think? Clearly articulate your response to this question.

III. Define the Terms

Write a definition for each of the following terms.

1. multicultural education (p. 86)

2. macroculture (p. 92)

3. microculture (p. 92)

4. ethnic group (p. 97)

5. exceptionality group (p. 97)

6. curriculum-based assessment (p. 103)

7. "dilemma of difference" (p. 103)

8. native language emphasis (p. 109)

9. sheltered English (p. 109)

10. scaffolded instruction (p. 109)

11. mnemonics (p. 109)

12. cooperative learning (p. 113)

IV. Know the Content in This Chapter

A. Matching

a) native language emphasis
b) macroculture
c) scaffolded instruction
d) multiculturalism
e) multicultural education
f) sheltered English
g) cooperative learning
h) reciprocal teaching
i) mnemonics
j) microcultures

1. ____ designed to change educational institutions and curricula so that they will provide equal educational opportunities to students regardless of their gender, social class, ethnic group, race, disability, or other cultural identity (p. 86).

2. ____ is now a specialized field of study and research in the field of education (p. 91).

3. ____ the result when the six major components of a culture come together and form a national culture (p. 92).

4. ____ smaller cultures that share the common characteristics of the larger culture but have unique values, styles, language and dialects, nonverbal communication, awareness, frames of reference and identity (p. 92).

5. ____ in this approach students are taught in their native language and later make the transition to English (p. 109).

6. ____ in this approach students receive instruction in English for most of the day from the beginning (p. 109).

7. ____ the teacher provides assistance to the student learning a task and then phases out the help as the student learns to use specific strategies independently (p. 109).

8. ____ the teacher models the use of a learning strategy and then the student tries it out (p. 109).

9.	___ the use of memory aids such as visual representations or rhymes (p. 109).

10.	___ one of the most effective ways of breaking down prejudice and encouraging appropriate interaction among students with different characteristics (pp. 112-113).

**B.	True or False**

1.	Multiculturalism is now a specialized field of study and research in education (p. 91). T or F

2.	An individual can belong to both a macroculture and a microculture (p. 92). T or F

3.	The number of microcultures represented in schools in the United States has decreased in recent decades (p. 92). T or F

4.	All students from microcultures within the United States perform rather poorly in school (pp. 92-93). T or F

5.	The community and the school both share a critical role in positive outcomes for children from diverse and multicultural backgrounds (p. 94). T or F

6.	Developing a positive attitude toward cultural groups different from one's own occurs naturally in most individuals (p. 95). T or F

7.	Ethnic or national origin is the most important dimension of cultural diversity (p. 95). T or F

8.	One of the most controversial aspects of multicultural education is the use of language (p. 95). T or F

9.	An individual could be identified as exceptional in one ethnic group but not in another (p. 97). T or F

10.	Students may be particularly likely to be identified or not identified as having a disability depending on their gender and ethnicity (p. 99). T or F

11. There is no evidence to support the belief that students from Black or Hispanic cultures are overrepresented in any particular disability category (p. 99). T or F

12. Typically, traditional assessment practices provide information that is useful in teaching (p. 101). T or F

13. Due to the possibility of unfairness, educational assessment can be misleading and is, therefore, damaging and unnecessary (pp. 101-103). T or F

14. A very effective method of helping to reduce prejudice and to promote healthy interactions among students with different characteristics is cooperative learning (p. 113). T or F

C. Fill in the Blank

1. A shared set of values, behavioral styles, language and dialect, and nonverbal communication which make up a national or shared culture is referred to as a _____ (p. 92).

2. Within a larger culture, smaller cultures that share common characteristics but also have their own unique values, styles, languages, and dialects are referred to as _____ (p. 92).

3. _____ is a method of assessment that involves students' responses to their usual instructional materials; it involves direct and frequent samples of performance on specific content area instruction (p. 103).

4. _____ is one of the most effective ways of breaking down prejudice and encouraging appropriate interaction among students with different characteristics (p. 112).

D. Multiple Choice

1. Which of the following factors contribute to the academic and social success of individuals from microcultures? (p. 93).
   a) values and beliefs   d) opportunities
   b) behavioral styles   e) all of the above
   c) attitudes and motivation

2.   Which of the following is *not* a way in which the community can provide encouragement for the academic success of an involuntary minority? (pp. 93-94).
   a)   Teach children that success can be obtained only within the school system.
   b)   Provide evidence that academic success is valued and appreciated in the community.
   c)   Provide successful role models.
   d)   Teach children responsibility for their academic success.

3.   Multicultural special education must focus primarily on: (p. 98)
   a)   ensuring that ethnicity is not mistaken for educational exceptionality
   b)   teaching students with disabilities to appreciate diversity
   c)   increasing understanding of the microculture of exceptionality and its relationship to other cultures
   d)   a and c only

4.   Individuals in minority ethnic groups are more apt to be identified as disabled because: (p. 98)
   a)   they do not use eye contact
   b)   they do not communicate effectively
   c)   their differences are not adequately understood and valued
   d)   their differences make them appear to be unable to function independently within society

5.   Cultural diversity presents particular challenges to special educators in all areas except: (p. 100)
   a)   assessment
   b)   instruction
   c)   program funding
   d)   socialization
   e)   overcoming students' prejudice and stereotyping

6.   The assessment practices of educators and psychologists have frequently been criticized as: (p. 98)
   a)   an overly expensive and lengthy process which provides no benefits to the child
   b)   biased, resulting in misrepresentation of the abilities and disabilities of ethnic minorities and exceptional children

c)	useless, resulting only in labeling or classification rather than improved educational programming
d)	both b and c
e)	both a and c

7.	Which of the following assessment methods provides useful information to teachers and can, in fact, reduce the cultural bias often associated with assessment? (pp. 98-102).
a)	standardized intelligence/achievement tests
b)	curriculum-based assessment
c)	instructional environment assessment
d)	both a and b
e)	both a and c

8.	The problems of assessing students to qualify for special education are related to which of the following: (p. 101)
a)	use of traditional standardized testing procedures
b)	failure to take cultural diversity into account
c)	focus on individual deficits alone
d)	no information is provided on how to teach the student
e)	all of the above

9.	It is important to teach a student from a microcultural group: (pp. 102-105)
a)	only skills valued by students' microcultures
b)	the language of the dominant culture while ignoring their native, now irrelevant, language
c)	using instruction which is geared to the individual cultural style of students
d)	teach skills students need to survive and prosper in the larger context of the macroculture

## E.	Short Answer

1.	What is the purpose of multicultural education? (p. 86).

2.	What two tasks may be accomplished if we adopt a multicultural perspective? (p. 86).

3. What is the reason for the increase in the number of microcultures in schools in the United States? (p. 92).

4. Discuss the difference between voluntary and involuntary minorities (p. 93).

5. What might explain why children from some diverse cultural backgrounds are not successful in schools in the United States? (p. 93).

6. Describe at least five basic dimensions of cultural diversity (p. 95).

7. Provide an example of a student who has a disability in an Anglo-dominant microculture and may not be identified as disabled in another microculture (p. 100).

8. What three objections are commonly expressed about the use of traditional standardized testing to assess students with disabilities? (p. 102).

9. What is the focus of an assessment of the instructional environment? What kinds of information become available through such an assessment? (p. 102).

10. What is the purpose of the alternative assessment procedures devised in the late 1980s and early 1990s? (p. 102).

11. How might curriculum-based assessment address cultural diversity within classrooms in the United States? (p. 103).

12. When teaching students with linguistic or cultural differences, it is not sufficient to be guided by the students' differences alone. Do you agree or disagree with this statement? Why? (pp. 103-105).

13. Do you support or reject the hypothesis that children from the African-American culture should be taught in a manner which highlights the African culture and seeks distinctively African modes of teaching and practice? Provide a clear rationale to explain your position (pp. 105-106).

14. Describe four instructional goals which educational reformers consider essential for the development of equality and fairness in education? (p. 107).

15. Briefly describe the six components of effective teaching practices which facilitate effective multicultural education? (pp. 109-111).

16. What are the educational implications (assessment, instruction, and socialization) of the current increase in microcultures within school systems across the United States? (pp. 92-116).

V. Enrichment Activities

1. Talk with the principal of a large urban school, a suburban school and a rural school and find out how many cultures are represented in each school. Then ask the principals how each faculty and staff address the unique assessment, instruction and socialization needs of the students.

2. What multicultural education issues were highlighted in the film *Stand and Deliver*. Describe each of these issues in detail. Reflect on how you would cope with these issues as a teacher.

Answer Key for Chapter Three

Matching	True or False	Multiple Choice
1. e	1. T	1. e
2. d	2. T	2. a
3. b	3. F	3. d
4. j	4. F	4. c
5. a	5. T	5. c
6. f	6. F	6. d
7. c	7. F	7. b
8. h	8. T	8. d
9. i	9. T	9. d
10. g	10. T	
	11. F	
	12. F	
	13. F	
	14. T	

Chapter 4

Mental Retardation

I. Important Points to Remember

* In many areas, children with mental retardation function like children without disabilities.

* Most children classified as mentally retarded are mildly retarded and look like the average child next door.

* A new definition of mental retardation was recommended by the American Association on Mental Retardation in 1992.

* Today's professionals believe that mental retardation is not necessarily a permanent condition.

* Based on the current definition, individuals with mental retardation require either pervasive, extensive, limited, or intermittent support.

* Public school administrators report that somewhere around 1 to 1.5 percent of schoolage children are officially identified as having mental retardation.

* The cause of mental retardation remains unknown among 85-90 percent of individuals.

* Today the causes of severe mental retardation are more readily traced, and not surprisingly, less is known about the causes of mild mental retardation.

* The results of intelligence and adaptive skills' assessments determine whether a person has mental retardation.

* The focus of educational programming varies according to the degree of students' mental retardation.

*   An academic focus is appropriate for students with a lesser degree of mental retardation, whereas self-help, community living, and vocational skills are the focus of educational programming for students with more severe mental retardation.

*   Early intervention programming is designed to help young children with mental retardation to achieve their highest cognitive level.

*   Transition programming addresses the development of community adjustment and employment skills.

II.   Reflection and Discussion

1.   "Today, professionals are more reluctant to apply the label of mental retardation than they once were" (p. 120). Is this a positive development? Support your conclusion with at least three convincing arguments.

2.   "... professionals have become more optimistic about the beneficial effects of educational programming. ...some persons with retardation, especially those with mild retardation, can eventually improve to the point that they are no longer classified as retarded" (p. 123). Are you surprised by this statement? What is your experience with the effects of educational programming?

3.   "The authors of the AAMR classification scheme believe [that] categorization based on support needed is better than categroization based on IQ ..." (p. 124). What rationale do they use to support this conclusion?

4.   "Today, however, most authorities hold that both genetics and the environment are critical determinants of intelligence" (p. 128). How would you argue if you were to take a stand in the nature versus nurture controversy? Explain your rationale.

5.   "There are several different types of Down syndrome, but the most common, by far, is trisomy 21" (p. 129). Are you surprised that little is communicated about the other types of Down syndrome? What is the advantage of the accumulation and dissemination of more information about Down syndrome?

6. "Even though employment statistics for workers who are retarded have been pessimistic, most professionals working in this area are optimistic about the potential for providing training programs that will lead to meaningful employment ..." (p. 148). Do you believe that there is sufficient grounds for this optimism? Defend your conclusions with examples.

III. Define the Terms

Write a definition of the following terms:

1. mental retardation (p. 122)

2. intellectual functioning (p. 122)

3. adaptive skills (p. 122)

4. cut-off score (p. 122)

5. levels of support (p. 124)

6. conceptual intelligence (p. 125)

7. practical intelligence (p. 125)

8. social intelligence (p. 125)

9. cultural-familial retardation (p. 127)

10. Down syndrome (p. 129)

11. Trisomy 21 (p. 129)

12. Williams syndrome (p. 130)

13. Fragile X syndrome (pp. 130-131)

14. Phenylketonuria (p. 131)

15. Tay-Sachs disease (p. 131)

16. encephalitis (p. 132)

17. microcephalus (p. 133)

18. hydrocephalus (p. 133)

19. fetal alcohol syndrome (p. 133)

20. anoxia (p. 134)

21. mental age (p. 135)

22. chronological age (p. 135)

23. self-regulation (pp. 137-138)

24. learned helplessness (p. 138)

25. readiness skills (p. 139)

26. functional academics (p. 139)

27. functional assessment (p. 144)

28. community residential facility (p. 145)

29. sheltered workshop (p. 150)

30. supported competitive employment (pp. 150-151)

IV.   **Know the Content in this Chapter**

A.   **Matching:**

      a)   functional academics
      b)   Penylketonuria
      c)   fetal alcohol syndrome
      d)   cultural-familial retardation
      e)   sheltered workshop
      f)   community residential facility
      g)   Fragile X

h) practical intelligence
i) social intelligence
j) Down syndrome

1. _____ the ability to maintain and sustain oneself as an independent person while managing the ordinary activities of daily living (p. 125).

2. _____ the ability to understand social expectations and the behavior of others and to judge how to conduct oneself in social situations (p. 125).

3. _____ mild mental retardation which no evidence of brain damage and mental retardation in a parent and a sibling (p. 127).

4. _____ results from trisomy 21, whereby the twenty-first set of chromosomes is a triplet rather than a pair (p. 129).

5. _____ is thought to be the most common hereditary cause of mental retardation (pp. 130-131).

6. _____ the inability of the body to convert phenylalanine to tyrosine, thereby causing abnormal brain development (p. 131).

7. _____ causes babies to be born with a variety of physical deformities as well as mental retardation (p. 133).

8. _____ involve learning to read a newspaper, use a telephone book, read labels on food and clothing items, make change and fill out job applications (p. 139).

9. _____ are alternatives to large institutions and accommodate three to ten people while under the direction of "house parents" (p. 145).

10. _____ is a structured environment where a person receives training and works with other workers with disabilities on jobs which require relatively low level skills (p. 150).

B. True or False:

1. It can be misleading to characterize even individuals with more severe mental retardation as helpless (p. 120). T or F

2. Institutionalization is the norm for individuals with severe mental retardation (p. 120). T or F

3. In most cases, we can identify the cause of mental retardation (p. 121). T or F

4. The cut-off score of 85 on an IQ test is used as an indicator of mental retardation (p. 123). T or F

5. Given appropriate education, individuals with mild mental retardation can improve their functioning to the point that they are no longer classified as retarded (p. 123). T or F

6. AAMR recommended that professionals classify students with mental retardation according to how much support they need to function as competently as possible (pp. 123-124). T or F

7. Intermittent, limited, extensive, or pervasive represent the levels of support needed by an individual with mental retardation (p. 124). T or F

8. Most individuals with mental retardation require pervasive support in order to function (p. 127). T or F

9. Down syndrome is estimated to account for 5-6 percent of all cases of mental retardation (p. 130). T or F

10. The likelihood of having a child with Down syndrome increases with the age of the mother (p. 129). T or F

11. Rubella, syphilis, and herpes simplex in the mother can cause retardation in a child (p. 132). T or F

12. Meningitis is the fastest growing infectious cause of mental retardation (p. 132). T or F

13. A blow to the head or child abuse can cause mental retardation (p. 133). T or F

14. Delayed or deviant language development is seldom evident in persons with mental retardation (p. 134). T or F

15. Available data supports the effectiveness of early intervention programming for young children at risk for disability and for those with disabilities (pp. 145-147). T or F

16. Almost 99 percent of individuals with mental retardation who graduate from high schools are employed (p. 149). T or F

17. Supported competitive employment offers potential problems for individuals with mental retardation (p. 151). T or F

18. Many individuals with mental retardation are achieving levels of independence in community living and employment that were never before thought possible (p. 151). T or F

C. Fill in the Blank:

1. With advanced methods of providing _____ and _____ training, people with mental retardation are capable of leading more independent lives than was previously thought possible (p. 120).

2. When workers with mental retardation fail on the job, it is usually because _____(pp. 121, 148).

3. Ability related to academic performance refers to _____ intelligence (p. 125).

4. _____ intelligence refers to abilities related to coping with one's environment (p. 125).

5. Persons with a mild degree of mental retardation who have no evidence of brain damage, at least one parent who is retarded, and one sibling who is retarded may have _____ (p. 127).

6.   The most common type of Down syndrome is _____ (p. 129).

7.   _____ that may lead to mental retardation can occur in the mother-to-be or the infant or young child after birth (p. 132)

8.   When using _____, the child learns academics in order to do such things as read a newspaper, read the telephone book, or make change (p. 139).

9.   _____ involves determining the consequences, antecedents, and setting events that maintain inappropriate behaviors (p. 144).

10.   Programs for preschoolers at-risk and those with disabilities place a great deal of emphasis on _____ and _____ (p. 147).

11.   The vocational training and employment approaches for individuals with mental retardation are usually delivered through either _____ or _____ (p. 149).

12.   A _____ is a structured environment where a person receives training and works with other workers with disabilities on jobs requiring relatively low skills (p. 150).

D.   Multiple Choice:

1.   Which of the following represents a reason why professionals are reluctant to apply the label of mental retardation? (pp. 120).
      a)   children from subcultural groups tend to score poorly on intelligence tests
      b)   labeling can cause children to develop poor self-concepts
      c)   mental retardation becomes apparent only in contained settings i.e. schools
      d)   all of the above

2.   Professionals rely on the assessment of two areas to indicate mental retardation. These areas are: (p. 122).

a) poor job skills and incompetence in task production
b) a low level of adaptive behavior and poor social skills
c) low intellectual functioning and low adaptive skills
d) a discrepancy between performance and IQ scores
e) none of the above

3. The current definition of mental retardation sanctions a cut-off score of: (p. 122).

a) 70-75
b) 65-70
c) 75-80
d) 80-85
e) none of these

4. In what percentage of individuals can experts determine the cause of mental retardation? (p. 126).

a) 90-95 percent
b) 50-60 percent
c) 10-15 percent
d) 80-85 percent
e) none of these

5. The cause of mental retardation is more readily known among individuals who need: (p. 127).

a) pervasive supports
b) intermittent supports
c) limited supports
d) intensive supports
e) none of these

6. Precisely what do professionals mean when they use the term cultural familial retardation? (p. 127).

a) no evidence of brain damage
b) at least one parent who is retarded
c) having one or more siblings who are retarded
d) all of the above

7. Which of the following may not be used to assess the intelligence of individuals with mental retardation? (pp. 135-136).

a) Kaufman Assessment Battery for Children
b) Wechsler Intelligence Scale for Children
c) Adaptive Behavior Scale - School Edition
d) none of the above

8. Professionals who work with students with mental retardation are cautioned not to place too much faith in IQ tests. Why? (p. 135).

a) IQ scores can change from one testing to another even when highly reliable tests are used.
b) All IQ tests are biased.
c) The younger the child the less valuable the test.
d) A superior IQ score does not guarantee a happy life.
e) All of the above are true.

9. Education programs for individuals with a lesser degree of mental retardation focus primarily on: (p. 138)
a) academic skills
b) self-help and community living skills
c) vocational skills
d) b and c only

10. The primary goal of preschool programs for children with disabilities is: (p. 147).
a) to reduce the probability that these children will be identified and classified as mentally retarded when they enter school
b) to improve the parenting skills of parents and/or guardians
c) to prevent the development of mental retardation
d) to help the children achieve as high a cognitive level as possible
e) to provide parents of children with mental retardation with a support group

11. Transition programming for students with mental retardation emphasizes: (p. 148).
a) academic and social skills
b) vocational skills
c) community adjustment and employment
d) none of the above

12. Data indicate that when individuals with mental retardation fail on the job, it is usually due to: (p. 148).
a) difficulty performing the job
b) inability to use automated equipment
c) job responsibility and social skills
d) inadequate vocational skills development

E. Short Answer:

1. What did Hallahan and Kauffman describe as a "radical departure" in the 1992 AAMR definition? (pp. 123-124).

2. The terms mild, moderate, severe, and profound are often used by school district personnel in program development for their students with these disabilities. What do these terms mean? (p. 123).

3. What are the two major criticisms of professionals who oppose the new AAMR definition (p. 124).

4. Write four different genetically related conditions involving mental retardation (pp. 128-131).

5. Describe the link between Down syndrome and Alzheimer's disease (p. 130).

6. Name three infections which can cause brain damage? (pp. 132-133).

7. What formal assessment instruments can be used to assess children's intelligence and adaptive behavior? (pp. 135-136).

8. Describe seven major psychological and behavioral characteristics of children with mental retardation (pp. 136-138).

9. List four readiness skills and state the intent of these skills (p. 139).

10. What are the characteristics of educational programs for students with severe mental retardation (pp. 139-144).

11. What is the purpose of functional assessment? (p. 144).

12. What two purposes do early intervention preschool programs serve? (p. 146).

F.   Enrichment:

1. How many convincing arguments can you make to support whether nature or nurture is the more critical variable? List all your arguments and note for which variable you can develop the largest number of convincing arguments?

2. Best Buddies is a student organization which is involved with developing age appropriate friendships between university students and adults with mental retardation. Is there a Best Buddies student organization on your campus? If so, find out how you might become involved. For more information, call Best Buddies headquarters at 305-374-2233.

3. Call a principle of a public elementary or high school and ask him/her to provide you with the name of a teacher who teachers with students who have mental retardation. Call this teacher and arrange a visit so that you may observe this educational program. Following your observation, talk with the teacher about the purpose of the program and how this relates to the students' future.

Answer Key for Chapter Four

Matching		True or False		Multiple Choice	
1.	h	1.	T	1.	d
2.	i	2.	F	2.	c
3.	d	3.	F	3.	a
4.	j	4.	T	4.	c
5.	g	5.	T	5.	d
6.	b	6.	T	6.	a
7.	c	7.	T	7.	c
8.	a	8.	F	8.	e
9.	f	9.	T	9.	a
10.	e	10.	T	10.	c
		11.	T	11.	c
		12.	F	12.	c
		13.	T		
		14.	F		
		15.	T		
		16.	F		
		17.	T		
		18.	T		

Chapter 5

Learning Disabilities

I. **Important Points to Remember**

* Children with learning disabilities have learning problems in school even though they may be no less intelligent than their nondisabled peers.

* Reading often looms as an area of particular difficulty to children with learning disabilities.

* During the preschool years children with learning disabilities may be inattentive and hyperactive.

* Children with learning disabilities have been called a variety of confusing labels such as minimally brain injured, slow learner, dyslexic, and perceptually disabled.

* Although agreement on what constitutes a learning disability has caused much confusion among professionals in the field, one definition is commonly accepted and the federal government endorses this definition.

* Government figures indicate that between 5 and 6 percent of students between six and seventeen years old have learning disabilities; however, since 1976-1977 the size of the learning disabilities category has more than doubled.

* The causes of learning disabilities fall into three general categories, namely, organic and biological, genetic, and environmental.

* Academic assessment of students with learning disabilities is most popularly done through the use of standardized achievement tests,

informal reading inventories, formative evaluation measures, and authentic assessment.

* Though students with learning disabilities exhibit a range of unshared observable characteristics, specific academic difficulties are an essential shared characteristic for this group of students.

* Educational researchers have developed a range of data-based, educational methods to facilitate the learning of students with learning disabilities.

* At this time little is known about how to assess, identify, or educate children with learning disabilities at the preschool level.

* A remarkable increase in data-based, transition programming may be observed during the last fifteen years. Transition programming is designed to facilitate positive postsecondary outcomes for students with disabilities.

II. Reflection and Discussion

1. "Boys outnumber girls about three to one in the learning disabilities category" (p. 167). Are you surprised by this? Why or why not?

2. "Researchers have found that identical twins are more concordant than fraternal twins for reading disabilities and speech and language disorders" (p. 169). What are the implications of this finding?

3. "One limitation to most standardized tests is that they cannot be used to gain much insight into *why* students have difficulty" (p. 170). Critique the use of standardized tests. What purpose(s) do they serve for students with learning disabilities?

4. "Persons with learning disabilities exhibit a great deal of interindividual and intraindividual variation" (p. 174). What are the implications of this statement for special education professionals?

5. "With regard to social uses of language--commonly referred to as pragmatics--students with learning disabilities are often inept in the production and reception of discourse" (p. 175). What are the

implications of these deficit areas? Do you believe that they are relevant? Why?

6. "Students with attention problems display such characteristics as distractibility, impulsivity, and hyperactivity" (p. 177). What behaviors are observable in a classroom relative to these characteristics?

III.   Define the Terms

Write a definition for each of the following terms.

1.   Minimal brain injury (p. 162)

2.   IQ-achievement discrepancy (p. 163)

3.   MRI (p. 167)

4.   CAT-scan (p. 167)

5.   PET-scan (p. 167)

6.   Standardized Achievement Tests (p. 170)

7.   Wechsler Individual Achievement Test (WIAT) (p. 170)

8.   formative assessment (pp. 170-171)

9.   curriculum-based assessment (p. 172)

10.   informal reading inventories (p. 172)

11.   authentic assessment (p. 173)

12.   phonological awareness (p. 175)

13.   visual perception deficits (p. 176)

14.   auditory perception deficits (p. 176)

15.   Attention deficit hyperactivity disorder (p. 177)

16. short-term memory (p. 177)

17. working memory (p. 177)

18. comprehension monitoring (p. 178)

19. locus of control (p. 179)

20. learned helplessness (p. 179)

21. cognitive training (p. 181)

22. self-instruction (pp. 181-182)

23. mnemonic strategies (p. 183)

24. scaffolded instruction (p. 183)

25. self-regulated strategy development (p. 183)

26. task-analysis (p. 184)

27. preacademic skills (p. 189)

28. transition (p. 190)

IV.   Know the Content in This Chapter

A.   Matching

a) authentic assessment
b) portfolios
c) IQ-achievement discrepancy
d) formative evaluation methods
e) phonological awareness
f) mnemonic keyboard method
g) transition planning
h) attention deficit hyperactivity disorder
i) metacognition
j) learned helplessness

1. ___ this means that the child is not achieving up to potential as usually measured by a standardized test (p. 163).

2. ___ directly measures individual students' behavior to keep track of their progress (pp. 170-171).

3. ___ an attempt to measure individual students' critical thinking and problem solving abilities in real life situations (p. 173).

4. ___ the ability to understand the rules of how various sounds go with certain letters to make up words (p. 175).

5. ___ one's understanding of the strategies available for learning a task and the regulatory mechanisms to complete the task (p. 178).

6. ___ a student who is unable to stick to a task very long, fails to listen to others, talks nonstop, and blurts out the first thing on his/her mind (p. 177).

7. ___ are a collection of samples of students' work over a period of time (p. 173).

8. ___ the tendency of students to give up because no matter how hard they try, they expect to fail (p. 179).

9. ___ is designed to help students with memory problems remember information by presenting pictorial representations of abstract concepts (p. 183).

10. ___ addresses educational programming for students with learning disabilities in order to prepare them for adulthood (p. 190).

B.   True or False

1. We now recognize that, in most cases, a learning disability is a life-long condition with which a person must learn to cope (p. 161). T or F

2. Some researchers have recommended abandoning the notion of an IQ-achievement discrepancy as a criterion for identifying learning disabilities (p. 163). T or F

3. The term brain dysfunction has come to replace the term brain injured or brain damaged (p. 164). T or F

4. Children with learning disabilities have deficits in the ability to perceive and interpret visual and auditory stimuli--the same as the visual and auditory acuity problems of children who are deaf and/or blind (p. 164). T or F

5. Perceptual and perceptual-motor exercises result in high reading achievement (p. 164). T or F

6. Learning disabilities can occur along with environmental disadvantage, mental retardation, or emotional disturbance; but for children to be considered learning disabled, their learning problems must be primarily the result of their learning disabilities (pp. 164-165). T or F

7. Children with learning disabilities constitute more than half of all students who receive special education (p. 166). T or F

8. In most cases, the cause of learning disabilities remains a mystery (p. 167). T or F

9. More children with learning disabilities have deficits in the area of mathematics rather than in the area of reading (p. 176). T or F

10. Training visual perceptual skills in isolation improves reading ability (pp. 176-177). T or F

11. Students with learning disabilities run a greater risk than their peers of having deficits in social skills (p. 178). T or F

12. Students with learning disabilities have an external rather than an internal locus of control (p. 179). T or F

13. Parents and professional organizations support the placement of all students with learning disabilities in full-inclusion settings (pp. 188-189). T or F

14. Very little preschool programming is available for children with learning disabilities (p. 189). T or F

C. Fill in the Blank

1. _____ is an attempt to assess students' critical thinking and problem solving abilities in real life situations (p. 173).

2. _____ are the hallmark of learning disabilities; if these are not observed, a learning disability does not exist (p. 174).

3. Academically, _____ in particular often looms as a major stumbling block to students with learning disabilities (p. 175).

4. A child with _____ is often unable to stick with one task for very long, fails to listen to others, talks nonstop, and blurts out the first thing on his/her mind (p. 177).

5. Problems in the areas of _____ dispose students with disabilities to misread social cues and misinterpret the feelings and emotions of others (p. 178).

6. When using _____ students are prompted to ask themselves questions such as, "What do I have to do?", "How can I solve this problem?" and "How am I doing?" (pp. 181-182).

7. The purpose of _____ is to develop a more concrete way of taking in information so that it will be easier for students to remember (p. 183).

8. _____ provides temporary support while students are learning a task. This support is gradually removed when the students perform the task independently (p. 183).

9. The _____ method focuses on the details of the instructional process, stressing a systematic analysis of the concepts being taught, rather than an analysis of the characteristics of the student (p. 184).

10. _____ involves breaking down academic problems into their component parts so that teachers can teach the parts separately, and they teach the students to put the parts together in order to demonstrate the larger skill (pp. 184-185).

11. _____ materials are among the most well-researched commercial programs available for students with learning disabilities (p. 185).

12. In the mid-1990s _____ is the most popular placement for students with learning disabilities (p. 188).

13. When we talk about testing preschool children for learning disabilities, we are really talking about _____ rather than _____ (p. 189).

14. _____ are behaviors that are needed for formal instruction to begin, such as identification of numbers, shapes and colors (p. 189).

15. Postsecondary programs for individuals with learning disabilities include _____, as well as _____, and _____ (p. 192).

D. Multiple Choice

1. When did the field of learning disabilities first receive recognition by the federal government? (p. 160).
   a)   1956   d)   1969
   b)   1962   e)   none of the above
   c)   1960

2. Which one of the following is *not* a reason the term "minimal brain injury" went out of favor in the field of learning disabilities? (p. 162).
   a)   In neurological examinations children with minimal brain injury are indistinguishable from their peers without disabilities.
   b)   This diagnosis was based on questionable behavioral evidence.

c)   This label offered little real help to teachers in planning and implementing treatment.

d)   Too many children qualified for special education services based on this diagnosis.

3.   How many different definitions of learning disabilities have enjoyed some degree of acceptance since the field's inception? (p. 163).

a)   5   c)   11   e)   2

b)   7   d)   17

4.   Most definitions of learning disability exclude children whose learning problems stem from all of the following *except*: (pp. 164-166)

a)   poverty, abuse, and neglect

b)   low IQ scores and poor academic performance

c)   poor reality orientation

d)   intrinsic learning problems because of a central nervous system dysfunction

e)   mental retardation, emotional disturbance, and cultural differences

5.   Which of these best represents federal government estimates of the percentage of students six to seventeen years of age who have learning disabilities? (p. 166).

a)   9-10 percent   d)   5-6 percent

b)   1-2 percent   e)   17-20 percent

c)   6-7 percent

6.   The following are types of educational tests often used in the field of learning disabilities, except: (pp. 170-173)

a)   authentic assessment

b)   standardized achievement tests

c)   informal reading inventories

d)   computerized axial tomographic scans

e)   formative evaluation measures

7.   These deficits are the hallmark of learning disabilities: (p. 175)

a)   social skills   c)   academic

b)   mathematics skills   d)   science

e)   reading skills

8. Which of the following represents the major approaches to the academic problems of students with learning disabilities? (p. 181).
   a) direct instruction and parent programming
   b) structure, stimulus reduction, and social skills programming
   c) behavior modification and physical exercise
   d) cognitive training and direct instruction
   e) medication and parent programming

9. This approach involves the following three components - changing thought processes, providing strategies for learning, and teaching self-initiative: (p. 181)
   a) self-instruction
   b) cognitive training
   c) direct instruction
   d) mnemonic instruction
   e) none of the above

10. Which of the following methods of instruction combines several cognitive training techniques including self-instruction, goal setting, self-monitoring, and scaffolded instruction? (p. 183).
   a) direct instruction
   b) cognitive training
   c) self-regulated strategy development
   d) metacognitive training
   e) reciprocal teaching

11. Why do many professionals believe that preschoolers should not be identified as having learning disabilities? (p. 189).
   a) This would increase the number of children receiving special education in a dramatic manner.
   b) The learning disability label would have a particularly negative impact on a preschool child.
   c) Learning disability implies deficits in academics and academics are not ordinarily taught in preschool programs.
   d) none of the above

12. Section 504 of the Rehabilitation Act requires: (p. 192)
   a) students with disabilities to disclose information about their disabilities in college and university settings
   b) that students with learning disabilities take specialized courses in reading and mathematics

c)   college and university personnel to make reasonable accommodations for students with disabilities so that they will not be discriminated against because of their disabilities

d)   the peers of students with learning disabilities to provide appropriate assistance in the specific areas in which they have difficulty

E.   Short Answer

1.   What four factors have historically caused considerable controversy in the quest for an acceptable definition of learning disabilities? (p. 163).

2.   Explain why most definitions of learning disabilities specify disorders not included in the definition (pp. 165-166).

3.   How are formative evaluation methods used to assess students with learning disabilities? What purposes do they serve? (pp. 170-172).

4.   How might a teacher observe the intraindividual variation of students with learning disabilities? (p. 174).

5.   Briefly describe some ways that memory, cognitive, and metacognitive problems impact the daily life of a person with a learning disability (pp. 177-178).

6.   How is cognitive training used in educational settings when teaching students with learning disabilities? (pp. 181-184).

7.   Cognitive training involves three components. Describe each component in your own words (p. 181).

8.   Provide a rationale for why self-instruction seems to help students with learning disabilities (p. 181).

9.   How does direct instruction differ from other methods of teaching students with learning disabilities? (p. 184).

10.   Why is the full-inclusion setting the most common form of educational service delivery for students with learning disabilities? (p. 188).

11.   Do you agree or disagree that students with learning disabilities should be educated in "full inclusion" settings? Defend your conclusions as convincingly as possible (p. 188).

12.   Children of preschool age seldom attend programs designed for students with learning disabilities. Why? (p. 189).

13.   Would you advocate for or against the use of the learning disabilities label for children at the preschool level? Define your position with convincing rationale (pp. 189-190).

V.   Enrichment Activities

1.   Analyze the definitions of learning disabilities established by the federal government and the National Joint Committee on Learning Disabilities. Examine these definitions sentence by sentence and explain the ways these definitions are similar and dissimilar. What are your suggestions for the improvement of the definition of learning disabilities?

2.   Talk with a teacher at either the elementary or secondary school level and ask him/her how and why he/she decided to become a teacher of children with learning disabilities. Ask what dimensions of this work he/she finds most rewarding. Consider other questions you would like to ask which would be of interest to you.

3. Read *Being Learning Disabled and a Beginning Teacher and Teaching a Class of Students with Learning Disabilities* by P. J. Gerber (1992) in <u>Exceptionality</u>, 3(4), 213-231. Evaluate how this teacher copes with his learning disability on a daily basis.

Answer Key for Chapter Five

Matching		True or False		Multiple Choice	
1.	c	1.	T	1.	d
2.	d	2.	T	2.	d
3.	a	3.	T	3.	c
4.	e	4.	T	4.	c
5.	i	5.	F	5.	d
6.	h	6.	T	6.	d
7.	b	7.	T	7.	c
8.	j	8.	T	8.	d
9.	f	9.	F	9.	b
10.	g	10.	F	10.	c
		11.	T	11.	c
		12.	T	12.	c
		13.	F		
		14.	T		

Chapter 6

Attention Deficit Hyperactivity Disorder

I.   **Important Points to Remember**

*   ADHD is not recognized as its own separate category by the US Department of Education; students with ADHD are served by special education under the category of "other health impaired".

*   ADHD is not a modern invention. In fact, scientific evidence indicates the existence of ADHD at the beginning of twentieth century.

*   William Cruickshank was one of the first to establish an education program for children who would meet today's criteria for ADHD.

*   From one-third to one-half of cases referred to guidance clinics are for ADHD, and most authorities estimate that 3-5 percent of the school-age population have ADHD.

*   Today psychological theorists believe that the essential impairment in ADHD is a deficit involving behavioral inhibition.

*   Current research indicates that ADHD most likely results from neurological dysfunction rather than from actual brain damage.

*   Scientists using neuroimaging techniques have found consistent abnormalities in three areas of the brain in persons with ADHD. These are the frontal lobes, basal ganglia, and the cerebellum.

*   Research evidence indicates that exposure to lead, and the abuse of alcohol or tobacco by pregnant women places an unborn child at increased risk for ADHD.

*   Currently researchers are attempting to tease out why ADHD co-occurs with so many other learning and behavioral disabilities.

*   Students with ADHD find it exceedingly difficult to stay focused on tasks that require effort and concentration.

*   Teachers have a wide array of data based behavior management procedures available to them when working with students with ADHD.

*.   Diagnosis of young children with ADHD is particularly difficult because many young children without ADHD exhibit similar behaviors.

*   ADHD often continues into adulthood and today some individuals are diagnosed with ADHD as adults.

*   Despite having ADHD, many adults have highly successful careers and many have happy marriages and families.

II.   Reflection and Discussion

1.   "… because ADHD is not recognized as a separate category of special education by the U.S. Department of Education, it is difficult to estimate how many students with ADHD are served in special education " (p. 208). Do you support the idea that ADHD should be a separate category of special education? Explain your perspective.

2.   "… boys may be over-identified as ADHD and/or … girls may be under-identified as ADHD" (p. 208). Do you believe that this is possible and probable? Why or why not?

3.   "Although authorities view the interview as essential to the diagnosis of ADHD, clinicians also need to recognize the subjective nature of the interview situation" (p. 211). Why might information from interviews be misleading?

4.   "… the invention of neuroimaging techniques … in the 1980s and 1990s allowed scientists for the first time to obtain more detailed and reliable measures of brain functioning…" (pp. 212-213). Describe the contributions and potential contributions of neuroimaging to our growing understanding of ADHD.

5. "...researchers have found consistent abnormalities in three area of the brain in persons with ADHD..." (p. 213). Do you believe that this is relevant information for teachers. Why or why not?

6. "...there is a growing consensus that inattention, as well as hyperactivity and impulsivity, are actually the result of problems in behavior inhibition" (p. 215). What are the implications of this information for parents and teachers?

7. "Not all professionals, parents, and laypeople are in favor of using Ritalin" (p. 227). What is your perspective on the use of Ritalin?

8. "...the majority of individuals diagnosed with ADHD in childhood will continue to have significant symptoms in adulthood" (p. 230). Describe at least four implications of this statement for educational programming for children and adults.

III. Define the Terms

Write a definition of each of the following terms:

1. Perseveration (p. 206)

2. Strauss syndrome (p. 206)

3. Minimal brain injury (p. 207)

4. ADHD (pp. 207-208)

5. Conners Teacher Rating Scale (pp. 211-212)

6. ADHD-Rating-Scale-IV (p. 212)

7. frontal lobe (p. 213)

8. basal ganglia (p. 214)

9. cerebellum (p. 214)

10. neurotransmitters (p. 214)

11. behavioral inhibition (p. 215)

12. executive functions (pp. 215-216)

13. inner speech (p. 215)

14. functional assessment (p. 224)

15. contingency-based self-management (pp. 224-225)

16. self-monitoring (p. 224)

17. psychostimulants (pp. 225, 227-229)

18. coaching (p. 235)

IV.   Know the Content in this Chapter

A.   Matching:

    a)   minimal brain injury
    b)   adaptive skills
    c)   William Cruickshank
    d)   Kurt Goldstein
    e)   contingency-based self-management
    f)   behavioral inhibition
    g)   frontal lobes
    h)   inner speech
    i)   coaching
    j)   basal ganglia

1.   ____ studied the psychological effects of brain injury in soldiers and observed figure-background confusion (p. 206).

2.   ____ was one of the first to establish an educational program for children who today would meet the criteria for ADHD (p. 207).

3.   ____ historically, a term used to describe children who had normal intelligence but who were inattentive, impulsive, and/or hyperactive (p. 207).

4.   ____ the front portion of the brain which is responsible for executive functions, such as, the ability to regulate one's own behavior (p. 213)

5.   ____ buried deep within the brain and are responsible for the coordination and control of motor behavior (p. 214).

6.   ____ the ability to withhold a response; to interrupt a response that has been stated; to protect an ongoing activity from interfering activities; and to delay a response (p. 215).

7.   ____ the inner "voice" that allows people to "talk" to themselves about various solutions when in the midst of solving a problem (p. 215).

8.   ____ are abilities needed to adapt to one's living environment (e.g. communication, self-care, home living, and social skills) (p. 216).

9.   ____ usually involve having persons keep track of their own behavior and then receive consequences, usually in the form of rewards, based on their behavior (p. 224).

10.   ____ involves identifying someone whom the person with ADHD can rely on for support (p. 235).

B.   True or False:

1.   ADHD is recognized as its own separate category such as learning disability and mental retardation in the United States (p. 204).
T or F

2.   Currently the <u>DSM</u> uses the general term ADD (p. 208). T or F

3.   Authorities in the early and mid-part of the twentieth century attributed problems of inattention and hyperactivity to neurological problems resulting from brain damage (p. 212). T or F

4.   Evidence points to heredity as playing a very strong role in the neurological dysfunction which causes ADHD (pp. 213-214). T or F

5. Studies indicate that if a child has ADHD, the chance of his/her sibling has ADHD is about 32 percent (p. 214). T or F

6. Complications at birth and/or low birth weight are associated with ADHD (p. 215). T or F

7. Persons with ADHD frequently have delayed inner speech (p. 215). T or F

8. Persons with ADHD run a lower risk for substance abuse than the general population (p. 218). T or F

9. Twenty five to 50 percent of persons with ADHD also exhibit some form of emotional or behavioral disorder (p. 217). T or F

10. Cruickshank's program is the most frequently used today - this involves a reduction of stimuli irrelevant in learning an a structured program with a strong emphasis on teacher direction (pp. 218-221).

11. A combination of functional assessment and contingency-based self-management techniques have proven successful in increasing appropriate behavior in elementary and secondary students with ADHD (pp. 218-221, 224-225). T or F

12. One of the most accepted treatments for ADHD is the use of psychostimulant medication (p. 225). T or F

C.   Fill in the Blank:

1. _____ is the tendency to repeat the same behaviors over and over again (p. 206).

2. The term _____ applied to children who had normal intelligence but who were inattentive, impulsive, and/or hyperactive (p. 207).

3. ADHD occurs much more frequently in _____than _____ (p. 208).

4. Several teams of researchers have found consistent abnormalities in three areas of the brain. These are _____, _____, and _____ (pp. 213-214).

71

5. Evidence for the generic transmission of ADHD comes from at least two sources (1)_____ and (2) _____ (p. 214).

6. _____ refers to the ability to withhold a planned response; to interrupt a response; to protect an ongoing activity from interfering activities; and to delay a response (p. 215).

7. _____ are those abilities needed to adapt to one's living environment (p. 216).

8. Studies have found an overlap of _____ percent between ADHD and learning disabilities (p. 217).

9. About _____ percent of individuals with Tourette's syndrome also have symptoms of ADHD (pp. 217-218).

10. Two aspects of effective educational programming for students with ADHD are _____ and _____ (p. 218).

11. _____ involves determining the consequences, antecedents, and setting events that maintain inappropriate behavior (pp. 224-225).

12. The teacher may teach students to use _____ to record how many times they left their seats during a class period (p. 224).

13. _____ is by far the most frequent type of psychostimulant prescribed for ADHD (p. 225).

14. Despite all the negative publicity in the media, most ADHD authorities _____ the use of psychostimulant medicine (p. 228).

15. _____ involves identifying someone whom the person with ADHD can rely on for support (p. 235).

D. Multiple Choice:

1. Who is credited for being one of the first authorities to bring the condition we now call ADHD to the attention of the medical profession? (p. 204).
   a) William Cruickshank
   d) Kurt Goldstein
   b) Heinz Werner and Alfred Strauss
   e) George F. Still

2. Goldstein reported that soldiers with brain injury were unable to concentrate perceptually and exhibited: (p. 206)
   a) poor attention
   b) figure-ground confusion
   c) conduct disorders
   d) associated disorders such as behavioral disorders and Tourette's syndrome
   e) substance abuse and poor peer relationships

3. William Cruickshank was one of the first to: (p. 207)
   a) establish an education program for children who today would meet the criteria for ADHD
   b) find out that children with cerebral palsy were more likely to respond to the background rather than the figure
   c) use Ritalin with children with ADHD
   d) establish the neurological base of ADHD
   e) a and b

4. The current DSM describes ADHD as: (p. 208)
   a) ADHD, Predominantly Inattentive Type
   b) ADHD, Predominantly Hyperactive-Impulsive Type
   c) ADHD, Combined Type
   d) a and b only
   e) a, b, and c

5. Which of the following best represents the estimated percentage of school-age students who have ADHD? (p. 208).
   a) 1-2 percent
   d) 3-5 percent
   b) 30-50 percent
   e) 15-20 percent
   c) 5-10 percent

6. Most authorities agree that there are three important components to assessing whether a person has ADHD. These are: (p. 208)
   a) personal history, medical examination and work products
   b) a clinical interview, completed teacher and parent rating scales, and a neurological examination
   c) a medical examination, a clinical interview, and teacher and parent rating scales
   d) informal behavioral ratings, work products, and classroom observations
   e) none of the above

7. The frontal lobes of the brain are responsible for: (p. 213)
   a) long- and short-term memory
   b) the ability to regulate one's own behavior
   c) behavioral inhibition
   d) chemicals sending messages between neurons in the brain
   e) control of motor behavior and movement

8. The basal ganglia and cerebellum are responsible for: (p. 214)
   a) behavioral inhibition
   b) coordination and control of motor behavior
   c) sending messages between neurons in the brain
   d) the ability to self-regulate
   e) long- and short-term memory

9. Behavioral inhibition refers to the ability to: (p. 215)
   a) control motor behavior and movement
   b) control inner speech
   c) withhold a planned response; to interrupt a response that has been started; to protect on ongoing activity from interfering activities; and to delay a response
   d) to keep information in the mind that can be used to guide one's actions either now or in the near future
   e) remember, have clear hindsight and forethought and have skills with time management

10. Individuals who have problems with working memory exhibit: (p. 215)
    a) inability to follow rules and instructions
    b) quick temper in frustrating situations
    c) forgetfulness, lack of hindsight, forethought, and problems

with time management
d) difficulty analyzing problems and communicating solutions to others
e) none of the above

11. The ability to engage in a variety of self-directed behaviors is referred to as: (p. 215)
a) behavioral inhibition
b) organizational skills
c) executive functions
d) inner speech
e) none of the above

12. ADHD often occurs simultaneously with which of the following conditions? (pp. 217-218).
a) behavioral and/or learning problems
b) learning disabilities
c) emotional or behavioral disorders
d) Tourette's syndrome
e) all of the above

13. According to Cruickshank, effective educational programs for children who today would meet the criteria for ADHD: (pp. 218-221, 224-225)
a) have a reduction of stimuli which are irrelevant to learning
b) enhancement of materials important to learning
c) a structured program
d) a strong emphasis on teacher direction
e) all of the above

14. Most authorities in the area of ADHD: (p. 228)
a) favor the use of Ritalin
b) oppose the use of Ritalin
c) are unsure how to regard the use of Ritalin
d) believe that Ritalin in the only intervention necessary for ADHD
e) none of the above

E.   Short Answer:

1. Describe the three important components which are used to assess whether a student has ADHD (pp. 208, 211-212).

2.   Describe the three areas of the brain in which researchers have found consistent abnormalities in persons with ADHD (pp. 213-214).

3.   Describe the role of behavioral inhibition in a classroom setting (p. 215).

4.   According to Barkley, in what ways do persons with ADHD exhibit problems with executive functions? (pp. 215-216).

5.   In what ways might a student in a classroom setting exhibit delayed inner speech? (pp. 215-216).

6.   Describe the characteristics of ADHD (pp. 215-218).

7.   Describe why some authorities have argued that the social problems experienced by students with ADHD should be the defining characteristics of the condition (pp. 216-218).

8.   Describe how students with ADHD exhibit coexisting conditions. What coexisting conditions might you expect these students to exhibit? (pp. 217-218).

9.   What are the two aspects of effective educational programming for students with ADHD? (pp. 218-221, 224-225).

10.   Describe how the psychostimulant, Ritalin effects ADHD (pp. 225, 227-229).

11.   Why is diagnosis of young children with ADHD particularly difficult? (pp. 229-230).

12.   What adult outcomes for individuals with ADHD most concern you? (pp. 232-235).

V.   Enrichment Activities

1.   Visit a classroom and observe how the teacher is working with students with ADHD - note the use of space, the teaching materials being used, the teacher's behaviors, and the teacher-student interactions. Note any other observations which came to your attention. Discuss the findings of your visit with a peer.

2.   There is frequent newspaper coverage of ADHD and related issues such as, the use of Ritalin. During the next few months, be attentive to any coverage you note in the newspapers you read. Observe and evaluate the quality of the coverage, in terms of its accuracy, relevance to family life, and educational programming.

Answer Key for Chapter Six

Matching		True or False		Multiple Choice	
1	d	1.	F	1.	d
2.	c	2.	F	2.	b
3.	a	3.	T	3.	e
4.	g	4.	T	4.	e
5.	j	5.	T	5.	d
6.	f	6.	T	6.	c
7.	h	7.	T	7.	b
8.	b	8.	F	8.	b
9.	e	9.	T	9.	c
10.	i	10.	F	10.	c
		11.	T	11.	c
		12.	F	12.	e
				13.	e
				14.	a

Chapter 7

Emotional or Behavioral Disorders

I. **Important Points to Remember**

*   Different terms have been used for children and youth with emotional or behavioral disorders; for example, in federal law they are referred to as emotionally disturbed, and among many professionals they are referred to as students with behavioral disorders.

*   Many professionals in the field prefer to use the term emotional or behavioral disorders.

*   Professionals continue to struggle with issues relative to the definition, classification, and identification of children and youth with emotional or behavioral disorders.

*   A new definition of emotional or behavioral disorders was proposed in 1990.

*   Researchers estimate that 6-10 percent of the school-age population have emotional or behavioral disorders; however, federal government estimates remain conservatively at 2 percent.

*   Only 1 percent of the school-age population are identified as having emotional or behavioral disorders, thus these students are largely underserved.

*   Biological, family, school, and cultural factors contribute to the development of emotional and behavioral disorders in children and youth.

*   A single cause is seldom attributed to the development of emotional or behavioral disorders.

*   Family disorganization, parental abuse, and inconsistent discipline are among the most important family factors which contribute to the development of emotional or behavioral disorders in children and youth.

*   Children and youth with emotional or behavioral disorders have particular difficulty with human relationships.

*   The behavioral characteristics of students with emotional or behavioral disorders range from withdrawn and isolated behaviors to acting out and violent behaviors.

*   In the school setting children and youth with emotional or behavioral disorders often have a history of school failure.

*   A range of educational theories, interventions, and placements are used by teachers of students with emotional or behavioral disorders.

*   Increasing numbers of students with emotional or behavioral disorders have poor academic outcomes, high dropout rates, and juvenile delinquency problems.

II.   Reflection and Discussion

1.   "Children and youths who have emotional or behavioral disorders are not typically good at making friends" (p. 246). Do you agree with this statement? What is your experience of children and youths with emotional or behavioral disorders?

2.   "Many different terms have been used to designate children who have extreme social-interpersonal and/or intrapersonal problems ...." (p. 248). Are you surprised by the lack of consensus on terminology?

3.   "Still, there is no universally accepted system for classifying emotional or behavioral disorders for special education" (p. 252). Would you recommend the development of a universally accepted classification system? Why or why not?

4. "Describing the characteristics of children and youths with emotional or behavioral disorders is an extraordinary challenge ...." (p. 264). Do you agree or disagree? Why?

5. "Children and youths with emotional or behavioral disorders tend to have multiple and complex needs" (p. 276). What might some of these "multiple and complex needs" be? What are the implications of this for special as well as general education teachers?

III. Define the Terms

Write a definition for each of the following terms.

1. emotionally disturbed (pp. 248-252)

2. externalizing behaviors (p. 252)

3. internalizing behaviors (p. 252)

4. conduct disorder (p. 252)

5. socialized aggression (p. 252)

6. schizophrenia (pp. 252-254)

7. autism (pp. 252-254)

8. pervasive developmental disorder (pp. 252-254)

9. Tourette's disorder (pp. 256-257)

10. three-step screening process (p. 263)

11. traumatic brain injury (TBI) (p. 269)

12. echolalia (p. 270)

13. neologism (p. 270)

14. self-stimulation (p. 270)

15. perceptual anomalies (p. 270)

16. apparent cognitive deficits (p. 270)

17. psychoeducational model (pp. 271-274)

18. behavioral model (pp. 274-276)

19. systematic, data-based interventions (p. 276)

20. multicomponent treatment (p. 276)

21. programming for transfer and maintenance (p. 277)

22. placement decisions (pp. 277, 280-281)

23. primary prevention (p. 284)

24. transition (pp. 286-287)

IV.   Knowing the Content in This Chapter

A.   Matching

    a)   emotionally disturbed
    b)   schizophrenia
    c)   conduct disorder
    d)   internalizing
    e)   externalizing
    f)   neologisms
    g)   traumatic brain injury (TBI)
    h)   echolalia
    i)   pervasive developmental disorder
    j)   autism

1.   _____ the term used when IDEA was enacted; this term has been criticized as inappropriate (pp. 248-249).

2.   _____aggressive, disruptive, antisocial behavior; this is the most common type of disorder exhibited by students who have been identified as having emotional or behavioral disorders (p. 253).

3. _____children with this disorder are often described as inaccessible to others, unreachable, out of touch with reality or mentally retarded (p. 253).

4. _____ children with this disorder have a severe thinking disorder. They may believe that they are controlled by alien forces or have other delusions or hallucinations. Typically their emotions are inappropriate for the actual circumstances and they tend to withdraw into a private world (pp. 253-254).

5. _____these children are characterized by lack of responsiveness to other people, major problems in communication, peculiar speech patterns, and bizarre responses, and these behaviors are usually observed before a child is three years old (pp. 253-254).

6. _____hitting, fighting, teasing, yelling, refusing to comply with requests, crying, destructiveness, vandalism, and extortion (pp. 265-267).

7. _____immature, withdrawn, infantile behaviors accompanied by a reluctance to interact with other people. These students are social isolates who have few friends and seldom play with children their own age (pp. 252, 267-269).

8. _____individuals with this disorder may exhibit violent aggression, hyperactivity, impulsivity, inattention, and a wide range of other emotional or behavioral problems (p. 269).

9. ____ made-up, meaningless words, or sentences - talk that bear little or no resemblance to reality (p. 270).

10. _____parroting what one hears and thereby using meaningless repetition, often misusing pronouns, e.g., "he" for "you", or "I" for "her" (p. 270).

B.   True or False

1. Children and youth with emotional or behavioral disorders typically have numerous friends among their peers and adults (p. 246).
    T or F

2.	The definition of "emotionally disturbed" includes a clause which states "the term does not include children who are socially maladjusted unless it is determined that they are seriously emotionally disturbed" (p. 250). T or F

3.	There is a universally accepted system for classifying emotional or behavioral disorders for special education (p. 252). T or F

4.	Most children with emotional or behavioral disorders escape the notice of their teachers (p. 262). T or F

5.	Children with E/BD tend to be particularly bright (p. 264). T or F

6.	Although children who are aggressive are a lot of trouble, they are not as seriously disturbed or disabled as children who are shy, anxious, or neurotic (p. 267). T or F

7.	Incarcerated youths with emotional or behavioral disorders are an especially neglected group in special education (p. 286). T or F

8.	The child or youth who is shy, anxious, or neurotic is most likely to have psychiatric problems as adult (p. 287). T or F

## C.	**Fill in the Blank**

1.	Numerous terms are used to describe children and youth with emotional or behavioral disorders. These terms do not refer to clearly different types of children and youth. Rather, the different labels appear to represent _____
_____(pp. 248-249).

2.	Write five reasons why arriving at a good definition of E/BD is particularly difficult (pp. 249-252).
	a)

	b)

	c)

	d)

e)

3. The definition of "emotionally disturbed" excludes children who
_____(p. 250).

4. Estimates of the prevalence of emotional or behavioral disorders in children and youths have varied tremendously because _____
_____(p. 254).

5. Teachers tend to overrefer students who exhibit _____
and underrefer students with _____(p. 263).

6. The emphasis of the _____ model is on intervention so that students gain insight that will result in behavioral change, rather than in changing the behavior directly (p. 271).

7. In the _____ model, the emphasis is on the behavior itself and behavior is a function of environmental events (p. 274).

D. Multiple Choice

1. Which statement best represents current thinking about how emotional and behavioral disorders start? (pp. 246, 248).
   a) These are the children and adolescents who frustrate, anger and irritate other people.
   b) The environment is so uncomfortable for some children and adolescents that they either withdraw or act out.
   c) The social interactions and transactions between the child and the social environment are inappropriate.
   d) The origins of emotional or behavioral disorders are unknown and no prevailing theory exists to explain them.
   e) None of the above are true.

2. Which one of the following does not represent common features comprising current definitions of emotional or behavioral disorders? (p. 250).
   a) emotional or behavioral disorders are intrinsic to individuals
   b) behavior that goes to an extreme
   c) a problem that is chronic

     d)   behavior which is unacceptable because of social and cultural expectations

     e)   all of above are common features of current definitions

3.   The most common types of problems exhibited by students with emotional or behavioral disorders are: (p. 251)
     a)   psychotic behaviors
     b)   hyperactivity and poor attention span
     c)   aggressive, acting-out disruptive behaviors
     d)   withdrawn and isolating behaviors
     e)   none of the above

4.   A particularly important aspect of immature, withdrawn behavior is: (pp. 252, 267-269)
     a)   aggression   d)   phobias
     b)   depression   e)   none of the above
     c)   anxiety

5.   Which of the following is *not* an example of socialized aggression? (p. 252).
     a)   physical aggression toward others
     b)   stealing in company with others
     c)   admitting disrespect for moral values and laws
     d)   loyalty to delinquent friends
     e)   none of the above

6.   Which of the following are characteristics of students with conduct disorders? (p. 252).
     a)   showing off and attention seeking
     b)   fights and temper tantrums
     c)   disruptive and annoying to others
     d)   all of the above

7.   Children with emotional or behavioral disorders mostly exhibit which one of the following behaviors? (pp. 252, 265-267).
     a)   depression   d)   externalizing
     b)   anxiety   e)   immaturity
     c)   psychosis

8. What is the federal government's often criticized conservative estimate of the number of schoolchildren in the United States who have emotional or behavioral disorders? (p. 254).
    a) 1 percent   d) 10 percent
    b) 2 percent   e) none of the above

9. Of the following, which contributes to the development of emotional or behavioral disorders? (pp. 255-262).
    a) family relationships
    b) biological disorders
    c) cultural expectations
    d) undesirable school experiences
    e) all of the above

10. In 1989 which organization was formed to help provide support and resources to caregivers of children with emotional and behavioral disorders? (p. 259).
    a) Council for Exceptional Children
    b) Council for Children with Behavioral Disorders
    c) The Federation of Families for Children's Mental Health
    d) The National Association for Caregivers of Children with Severe Behavioral Disorders
    e) none of the above

E. Short Answer

1. The National Mental Health and Special Education Coalition proposed a new definition of emotionally disturbed. What are the advantages of this newly proposed definition? (pp. 248-249).

2. Describe the four major factors which are attributed to the development of emotional or behavioral disorders (p. 255).

3. Describe the three-step screening process used by teachers to make certain that children who need special education services will not be overlooked? (p. 263).

4.	Describe at least five of the seven elements presented by the Peacock Hill Working Group which indicate quality education programming for students with emotional or behavioral disorders (pp. 276-277).

5.	Differentiate between autism, schizophrenia, and developmental disabilities (p. 270).

6.	How do professionals identify preschool children who are at high risk of developing emotional or behavioral disorders? (pp. 283-286).

## V.	Enrichment Activities

1.	Read *I Can Hear the Mourning Dove* by J. W. Bennett (Scholastic, 1993). Evaluate how the school personnel responded to Grace. Characterize how her teachers responded to her. How did her peers treat her? Do you believe that Luke's friendship was a positive influence in her life? Why or why not? What individual in her life responded most appropriately to her needs? What aspects of this book did you like most? Were there any aspects you disliked?

2.	Read *Dakota Dream* by J. W. Bennett (Scholastic, 1994). How did Floyd's teachers respond to Floyd's struggle with his identity? In what ways did this book influence the way you think about school personnel and institutions such as schools and hospitals? What are your overall comments about the contribution of this book?

3.	Talk with a special education teacher who works with children who have emotional or behavioral disorders at the elementary or high school level. Find out what attracted this teacher to the field of special education, and particularly, what attracted him/her to work with children who have behavioral disorders. Finally, ask this teacher to tell you about the child he/she believes made the most progress in his/her classroom. Are there any other questions you would be particularly interested in asking this teacher?

Answer Key for Chapter Seven

Matching		**True or False**		**Multiple Choice**	
1.	a	1.	F	1.	c
2.	c	2.	T	2.	a
3.	i	3.	F	3.	c
4.	b	4.	F	4.	b
5.	j	5.	F	5.	a
6.	e	6.	F	6.	d
7.	d	7.	T	7.	d
8.	g	8.	F	8.	b
9.	f			9.	e
10.	h			10.	c

Chapter 8

Communication Disorders

I. Important Points to Remember

*   Communication always involves a sender and a receiver of messages but it does not always involve language.

*   Speech-language therapy is one of the most frequently provided related services for children with other primary disabilities, such as, mental retardation, learning disability, and emotional or behavioral disorder.

*   There is a great variability in the age at which children may demonstrate a particular level of speech or language performance.

*   Rather than speech disorders, today speech-language pathologists are more concerned with language disorders.

*   Effective language intervention occurs in the child's natural environment and involves parents and classroom teachers, not just the speech-language pathologist.

*   A child may not have a speech or language disorder, yet he/she may have a culturally based communicative difference that demands special teaching.

*   Current trends in early intervention are directed toward providing speech and language intervention in the typical environments of young children.

*   Today it is recognized that most school and social difficulties of adolescents and adults are related to basic disorders of language.

*   Classroom teachers are in a particularly good position to identify language related problems and to request assistance from a communication specialist.

II.   Reflection and Discussion

1.   "Not all communication disorders involve disorders of speech" (p. 296). Precisely what do the authors mean by this statement? Provide an example to illustrate this point.

2.   "Speech and language are tools used for communication" (p. 296). Differentiate between speech, language, and communication using appropriate examples.

3.   "Mixed factors are included because language disorders often have multiple causes--combinations of central, peripheral, and environmental or emotional factors" (p. 300). In your own words, explain how some children might have language disorders which are causally associated with a set of "mixed factors."

4.   "The increasing inclusion of children with all types of disabilities in general education means that all teachers must become aware of how they can address language problems in the classroom" (p. 307). Are you surprised by this statement? Consider at least three major implications of this statement?

5.   "Preschoolers who require intervention for a speech or language disorder occasionally have multiple disabilities that are sometimes severe or profound" (p. 329). How would you explain the implications of this statement to a peer who is unfamiliar with the field of special education and communication disorders?

III.   Define the Terms

Write a definition for each of the following terms.

1.   communication (p. 296)

2.   communication disorders (p. 296)

3.   augmentative communication (pp. 298, 317-319, 322)

4.	speech disorders (pp. 298, 325)

5.	language disorders (p. 298)

6.	articulation (p. 298)

7.	fluency (p. 298)

8.	phonology (p. 298)

9.	morphology (p. 298)

10.	syntax (p. 298)

11.	semantics (p. 298)

12.	pragmatics (p. 298)

13.	specific language impairment (p. 306)

14.	early expressive language delay (p. 306)

15.	echolalia (p. 308)

16.	prelinguistic communication (p. 310)

17.	acquired aphasia (p. 311)

18.	augmentative communication (pp. 317-319, 322)

19.	facilitated communication (pp. 319, 322)

20.	voice disorder (p. 326)

21.	articulation disorder (pp. 326-327)

22.	fluency disorders (pp. 327-328)

23.	dysarthria (p. 328)

24.	apraxia (p. 328)

IV.   Know the Content in This Chapter

A.   Matching

   a)   augmentative communication
   b)   delayed language development
   c)   specific language impairment
   d)   acquired aphasia
   e)   milieu teaching
   f)   early expressive language delay
   g)   facilitated communication
   h)   prelinguistic communication

1.   ___ refers to language disorders that have no identifiable cause (p. 306).

2.   ___ refers to a significant lag in expressive language that the child will not "outgrow" (p. 306).

3.   ___ describes a child who progresses through the states of language development at a significantly later age than his/her peers (p. 309).

4.   ___ involves the use of gestures and vocal noises to request objects or greet (p. 310).

5.   ___ is naturalistic language intervention which is designed to teach functional language skills (p. 310).

6.   ___ is a loss of ability to understand and formulate language due to brain injury (p. 311).

7.   ___ refers to methods of communication for individuals who are unable to communicate effectively through speech because of a physical impairment (pp. 317-319, 322).

8.   ___ refers to a method of providing physical assistance to an individual while typing a message on a keyboard or in pointing to items on a communication board (pp. 319, 322).

B.   True or False

1.   Stuttering is the most common speech disorder (p. 296). T or F

2.   Those who use augmentative communication systems may or may not have language disorders in addition to their inability to use speech (p. 298). T or F

3.   Federal data indicate that about one million children receive services primarily for speech or language disorders (p. 298). T or F

4.   Environmental and emotional factors, such as, childhood neglect and abuse and behavioral and emotional problems, are associated with the language disorders of some children (p. 300). T or F

5.   There is a glut of speech-language pathologists in the schools (p. 300). T or F

6.   The underlying mechanisms that control the development of language are still not well understood (p. 301). T or F

7.   Language learning depends on brain development and proper brain functioning (p. 301). T or F

8.   The physiological, cognitive and social dimensions of learning language are clearly established and well understood in the professional community (p. 301). T or F

9.   Difficulty in either phonology, morphology, syntax, semantics, or pragmatics is virtually certain to be accompanied by difficulty with one or more of the others (p. 303). T or F

10.   The primary features of autism include impairments of social interaction and communication (p. 308). T or F

11.   Helping children to overcome speech and language disorders is the responsibility of speech-language pathologists alone (p. 313). T or F

12. Voice disorders can result from a variety of biological and nonbiological causes (p. 326). T or F

13. Lack of ability to articulate speech sounds correctly can be caused by biological factors (p. 327). T or F

14. If a child misarticulates only a few sounds consistently and suffers mild social rejection, an intervention program is not necessary (p. 327). T or F

C. Fill in the Blank

1. Speech and language are the tools of _____ (p. 296).

2. _____ is an arbitrary system of symbols, used according to rules, which communicate meaning (p. 298).

3. Speech disorders are impairments in the production and use of _____ (p. 298).

4. _____ involves an immediate or later parrot-like repetition of words or phrases heard (p. 308).

5. Teaching students functional language skills using naturalistic language intervention is known as _____ (p. 310).

6. A loss of ability to understand and formulate language due to brain injury is often referred to as _____ (p. 311).

7. _____ system must be designed for individuals who have physical or cognitive disabilities which preclude their development of communication using normal speech (p. 317).

8. _____ disorders are observed in individuals who have problems in the areas of pitch, loudness, or quality (p. 326).

9. When individuals omit, substitute, distort, or add word sounds they demonstrate _____ disorders (p. 326).

10. When individuals speak too fast, pause at the wrong place in a sentence, stumble, backtrack, or repeat syllables or words, they demonstrate _____ disorders (pp. 327-328).

11. _____ involves problems articulating speech sounds because of impaired control of muscle functioning (p. 328).

12. _____ is observed among individuals who have problems selecting and sequencing speech (p. 328).

D. Multiple Choice

1. Which of the following statements represents accurate information about communication disorders? (p. 296).
   a) Communication disorders carry social penalties.
   b) Disorders in communication do not always yield to intuitive or common sense "solutions."
   c) Communication is among the most complex human functions.
   d) All of the above are true.

2. Central factors are commonly associated with childhood language disorders. Which of the following is *not* referred to as a central factor? (p. 300).
   a) mental retardation
   b) neglect and abuse
   c) attention deficit hyperactivity disorder
   d) autism
   e) specific learning disability

3. What peripheral factors are associated with language disorders? (p. 300).
   a) hearing   d) physical
   b) visual   e) all of these
   c) deaf-blindness

4. What aspects of human development are commonly attributed to the development of language? (p. 301).
   a) behavioral   d) both b and c
   b) physical maturation   e) both a and b
   c) socialization and cognitive development

5.   Speech disorders include: (p. 325)
     a)   disorders of articulation and communication
     b)   language and voice disorders
     c)   disorders of voice, articulation, and fluency
     d)   disorders of pitch, loudness, and quality
     e)   none of the above

6.   When a speech pathologist is evaluating a child's voice, he/she is looking out for: (p. 326)
     a)   stuttering
     b)   problems in voice quality, resonance, pitch, and loudness
     c)   scratches on the larynx
     d)   psychological problems
     e)   infections of the tonsils, adenoids, or sinuses

7.   Lack of ability to articulate speech sounds can be caused by: (p. 327)
     a)   damage to the nerves involved with speech
     b)   loss of teeth
     c)   abnormalities of the oral structures, such as cleft palate
     d)   hearing loss
     e)   all of the above

8.   A child who speaks too fast to be understood, pauses at the wrong place in a sentence, stumbles and backtracks, and fills in pauses with "uh" while trying to think of what to say next demonstrates: (pp. 327-328)
     a)   fluency disorder   d)   communication disorder
     b)   articulation disorder   e)   none of the above
     c)   voice disorder

9.   What disability area most frequently accounts for dysarthria and apraxia? (p. 328).
     a)   learning disabilities   c)   behavioral disorders
     b)   mental retardation   d)   cerebral palsy

10. The inability to move the muscles involved in speech is known as: (p. 328)
     a)   dysarthria   d)   speech disorder
     b)   apraxia   e)   a and b only
     c)   articulation

E. Short Answer

1. Provide specific reasons why establishing the prevalence of communication disorders is a difficult task (pp. 298-300).

2. Do you expect that communication disorders will increase in the coming decades? Why or why not? (pp. 298-300).

3. Hallahan and Kauffman describe six theories of language development. Select the theory which most appeals to you and state the reason(s) for your selection (pp. 301-303).

4. When assessing a child's language, what two areas do evaluators focus on? Describe the procedures they use to evaluate these areas (pp. 306-308).

5. Who can be particularly helpful to children who are developing their speech/language skills? In what ways can they help? (pp. 313-316).

6. Some augmentative or alternative communication systems are more effective than others. What are the indicators of the effectiveness of these methods and devices? (pp. 317-319, 322).

7. The classroom teacher is primarily concerned with language disorders versus speech disorders. Why? (pp. 325-329).

8. What is the difference between voice disorders and articulation disorders? (pp. 326-327).

9. All children make articulation and phonological errors. When do these errors constitute a disorder? (pp. 326-327).

10. In what ways might chronic stuttering affect an individual's later life adjustment? (p. 328).

11. When a child is referred for problems in speech and language, what specific areas will the speech-language pathologist assess? (pp. 328-329).

12.	The first years of a child's life are a critical period for language learning. What can caregivers do to encourage a child's language development? (p. 329).

13.	In the past, adolescents and adults in speech and language intervention programs generally fell into three categories. Describe these three categories (pp. 331-333).

14.	What purposes can transition programs serve for adolescents and adults with speech and language disorders? (pp. 331-333).

## V.	Enrichment Activities

1.	Make an appointment to speak with a speech-language pathologist about his/her life as a professional. Ask him/her to tell you why he/she selected this profession. Then ask this individual to identify and discuss the most and least satisfying aspects of his/her profession.

2.	Talk with an individual who has received speech therapy. Find out what presenting problems initially led to an evaluation of speech and language. Then ask this individual to reflect on the impact of the communication disorder in his/her life. Finally, ask this individual to tell you about the person who was most important in his/her life relative to dealing with this disorder.

3.	For an audience of future special educators, develop an audio tape designed to provide examples of the various speech/language disorders which are described in this chapter.

Answer Key for Chapter Eight

Matching		True or False		Multiple Choice	
1.	c	1.	F	1.	d
2.	f	2.	T	2.	b
3.	b	3.	T	3.	e
4.	h	4.	T	4.	d
5.	e	5.	F	5.	c
6.	d	6.	T	6.	b
7.	a	7.	T	7.	e
8.	g	8.	F	8.	a
		9.	T	9.	d
		10.	T	10.	e
		11.	F		
		12.	T		
		13.	T		
		14.	F		

Chapter 9

Hearing Impairment

I.   Important Points to Remember

*   Many people with hearing impairments have problems with language development and communication in the dominant language of the hearing society.

*   The earlier a hearing loss manifests itself in a child's life, the more difficulty he/she will have developing the dominant language of the hearing society.

*   Because of individual differences, it is best not to form any hard and fast opinions about an individual's ability to hear and speak on the basis of a hearing disability classification.

*   Childhood deafness is most often caused by hereditary factors.

*   Some authorities believe that many children who are hard of hearing could benefit from special education, and currently they are not being served.

*   Estimates of the numbers of children with hearing impairments vary considerably.

*   Most children with hearing impairments have extreme deficits in achievement, particularly in the area of reading.

*   Many people who are deaf believe in the value of having their own Deaf culture.

*   Members of the Deaf community have their own cultural standards and their own preferences for specific educational and medical procedures.

*   Many of the most controversial issues surrounding early childhood intervention with students who are deaf focus on language.

II.   Reflection and Discussion

1.   "The oral versus manual debate has raged for centuries" (p. 342). How would you explain the perspectives of oralists versus manualists to an audience who is unfamiliar with this controversy?

2.   "... there is growing sentiment among people who are deaf that deafness should not even be considered a disability" (p. 345). Are you surprised by this? Why or why not?

3.   "... in terms of functioning in an English language-oriented society, the person who is deaf is at a much greater disadvantage than someone who is blind" (p. 351). Do you agree that a person who is deaf is at a greater disadvantage than a person who is blind? Provide at least three reasons to support your conclusions.

4.   "... professionals believed that the conceptual ability of individuals who are deaf was deficient because of their deficient spoken language" (p. 352). Are you surprised by this? How did the authors explain this development?

5.   "... more and more professionals agree with the many people who are deaf who believe in the value of having their own Deaf culture" (p. 354). Do you support the growing acceptance of the Deaf culture? Explain your perspective.

III.   Define the Terms

Write a definition for each of the following terms.

1.   total communication (pp. 342, 362)

2.   American Sign Language (ASL) (pp. 343, 363)

3.   decibels (p. 344)

4.   hearing impairment (p. 344)

IV.   Know the Content in This Chapter

A.   Matching

    a)   conductive hearing impairment
    b)   sensorineural hearing impairment
    c)   mixed hearing impairment
    d)   atresia
    e)   congenital cytomegalovirus (CMV)
    f)   American sign language
    g)   total communication
    h)   profoundly deaf
    i)   postlingual deafness
    j)   speech reading
    k)   fingerspelling
    l)   signing English systems

1.   _____ involves the blend of oral and manual techniques (pp. 342, 362-363).

2.   _____ asserted as a true language, with its own word order and considered the natural language of people who are deaf (pp. 343, 363-365).

3.   _____ a hearing threshold at 90 decibels and above (p. 344).

4.   _____ deafness occurring at any age following the development of language (p. 344).

5.   _____ refers to an impairment that interferes with the transfer of sound along the conductive pathway of the middle or outer ear (p. 349).

6.   _____ involves problems in the inner ear (p. 349).

7.   _____ results when the external auditory canal does not form (p. 349).

8.   _____ a combination of impairments involving the transfer of sound along the conductive pathway of the middle or outer ear and problems with the inner ear (p. 349).

9.   ____ the most frequent viral infection in children. This can cause visual or hearing impairment and mental retardation (p. 351).

10.   ____ involves teaching children who have hearing impairments to use visual information to understand what is being said to them (pp. 359, 362).

11.   ____ refer to approaches that professionals have devised for teaching people who are deaf to communicate (pp. 362-363).

12.   ____ the representation of letters of the English alphabet by finger positions and may also be used to spell out words (p. 363).

B.   True or False

1.   A hearing loss can affect an individual's ability to speak and develop language (p. 344). T or F

2.   The ear is one of the simpler and least complex organs of the body (p. 346). T or F

3.   It is now possible to test the hearing ability of infants within the first three months of life (p. 348). T or F

4.   A hearing loss that is greater than 60 or 70 decibels usually involves the inner ear (p. 349). T or F

5.   Childhood deafness is most commonly the result of accidents (p. 350). T or F

6.   Data indicate that very little interaction occurs between students who are deaf and those who are not (p. 354). T or F

7.   Over 90 percent of children who are deaf have hearing parents (p. 354). T or F

8.   Members of the Deaf culture argue for full integration of students who are deaf into general education classrooms (pp. 366-368). T or F

9. All children with hearing impairments benefit from the use of hearing aids (pp. 368-370). T or F

10. Parents who are deaf are better able to cope with their child's deafness (pp. 371-373). T or F

C. Fill in the Blank

1. The intensity of sound is measured in _____(p. 344).

2. A technique called _____ has been developed to test a person's detection and understanding of speech (p. 348).

3. The determination of the decibel levels at which one is able to understand speech is known as _____ (p. 348).

4. The most severe hearing impairments are associated with the _____ ear (p. 350).

5. _____ tests rather than verbal tests, especially if they are administered in sign, offer a much fairer assessment of the IQ of a person with a hearing loss (p. 352).

6. _____ is an approach to teaching students with hearing impairments that blends oral and manual techniques (p. 359).

7. _____ is the combination of oral and manual methods (p. 359).

8. _____ is a method of augmenting speechreading using hand shapes in order to represent sounds (p. 362).

9. _____ approach consists of using ASL as the primary language in academic instruction and English as the second language (p. 363).

10. The representation of letters of the English alphabet by finger positions is called _____(p. 363).

D. Multiple Choice

1. Total communication refers to: (pp. 342, 359, 362)
    a) the use of both oral and manual methods of communication
    b) the use of verbal, nonverbal, and body language
    c) the use of technology and available hardware and software
    d) the use of technology and other useful instruments along with the human voice
    e) none of the above

2. Educators are most concerned about: (p. 344)
    a) the decibel level of the hearing loss
    b) the physiological contribution to the deafness
    c) the effect of the hearing loss on language development
    d) the age of onset of the hearing impairment
    e) both c and d

3. Mild deafness is observed in individuals with a hearing threshold classification of: (p. 344)
    a) 10-20 decibels   d) 55-69 decibels
    b) 90 decibels and above   e) none of the above
    c) 26-54 decibels

4. Individuals with a threshold of 90 decibels and above have: (p. 344)
    a) profound deafness   d) 55-69 decibels
    b) mild deafness   e) none of the above
    c) moderate deafness

5. According to the US Department of Education, what is the estimated number of six to seventeen year olds identified as deaf or hard of hearing? (p. 345).
    a) 5 percent   d) .14 percent
    b) 1 percent   e) none of the above
    c) .5 percent

6. How do authorities explain that children who are deaf and who have parents who are deaf have higher reading achievement than those who have hearing parents? (pp. 353-354).
    a) Children who are deaf and who use ASL are usually more intelligent than children who are not deaf.

b) Parents who are deaf are able to communicate better with their children who are deaf through the use of ASL.
c) Parents and children who are deaf are more likely to be proficient in ASL and ASL aids in learning written English and reading.
d) both b and c

7. Which teaching technique is designed to encourage the child to use what hearing he/she possesses? (p. 359).
a) the total communication approach
b) auditory-verbal approach
c) American sign language
d) speech audiometry
e) none of the above

8. Those who advocate for the use of ASL often approach the education of children who are deaf from a bilingual perspective. Their rationale is that: (p. 363)
a) this approach best enhances students' academic performance
b) students who are deaf need a foundation in their natural language so It can servo as a basis for teaching them spoken English
c) many children who are deaf come from Hispanic homes
d) both a and b

9. A relay service for use by people with TTYs is mandated in all states. What is the advantage of relay services? (pp. 370-371).
a) Relay services are used in the education of students who are deaf.
b) Relay services enhance the total communication approach.
c) Relay services allow the person with the TTY to communicate with anyone through an operator who conveys the message to the person who does not have a TTY.
d) none of the above

10. In which area does most controversy exist relative to early intervention programming for preschoolers who are deaf? (p. 371).
a) language development   d) ASL
b) parent training   e) total communication
c) academic versus functional skills

E. Short Answer

1. Explain the differences between deaf and hard of hearing (p. 344).

2. Describe one reason why estimates of the numbers of children with hearing impairments vary (pp. 345-346).

3. Describe the major components and the function of the outer ear (p. 346).

4. Distinguish between the functions of the outer ear, middle ear, and inner ear (pp. 346-347).

5. Why are some children considered hard-to-test? (pp. 348-349).

6. What are the three major classifications professionals use to classify the causes of a hearing loss? (p. 349).

7. Differentiate between external otitis, otitis media, and nonsupperative otitis media (pp. 349-350).

8. Why is it much more difficult for children who are prelingually deaf to learn to speak than for those who have acquired their deafness later in their lives? (pp. 351-352).

9. Describe your understanding of the Deaf culture. Do you support the development of the Deaf culture? Why or why not? (pp. 354-355, 357).

10. How would you describe the controversy surrounding cochlear implants to someone who is unfamiliar with them? (pp. 357, 358).

V. Enrichment Activities

1. Read *Deaf Like Me* by T. S. Spradley and J. P. Spradley (Gallaudet University, 1985). What is the major contribution of this text to both individuals with and individuals without hearing impairments?

2. How is your own hearing? Consider a visit to an audiologist to have your hearing checked. Obtain specific data about your hearing levels.

3. Consult with the principal of a local elementary or high school and the director of student services at a local university. Find out what services are available for students who have hearing impairments in each setting. Compare the services which are available for students in each setting and outline a set of recommendations you would make to future administrators.

Answer Key for Chapter Nine

Matching		True or False		Multiple Choice	
1.	g	1.	T	1.	a
2.	f	2.	F	2.	e
3.	h	3.	T	3.	c
4.	i	4.	T	4.	a
5.	a	5.	F	5.	d
6.	b	6.	T	6.	d
7.	d	7.	T	7.	b
8.	c	8.	F	8.	b
9.	e	9.	F	9.	c
10.	j	10.	T	10.	a
11.	l				
12.	k				

Chapter 10

Visual Disabilities

I.   **Important Points to Remember**

*   Blindness is one of the least prevalent of all disabilities and it is much more common among adults than among children.

*   The majority of people who are blind can actually see.

*   The legal definition of visual impairment focuses on acuity while the educational definition focuses on how well individuals use functional skills.

*   The Snellen chart, consisting of rows of letters or rows of Es arranged in different positions, measures visual acuity for far distances.

*   Most authorities believe that lack of vision does not have a very significant effect on the ability to understand and use language.

*   Several intelligence tests for individuals with visual impairments are now available and they assess spatial and tactual skills.

*   Persons who are blind rely largely on tactual and auditory information to learn about the world.

*   Neither low academic achievement nor poor social adjustment are inherent conditions of blindness.

*   In school, students who have little or no sight usually require special modifications in the areas of Braille, use of remaining sight, listening skills, and mobility training.

* Today most students with visual disabilities receive their education in general education classrooms with the support services of an itinerant teacher.

* Professionals are eager to begin intensive early intervention as soon as possible with infants who have visual impairments.

II. Reflection and Discussion

1. "Blindness is primarily an adult disability. Most estimates indicate that blindness is approximately one-tenth as prevalent in school-age children as in adults" (p. 388). Why do you think that blindness is more prevalent among adults than among children?

2. "Persons who are blind rely much more on tactual and auditory information to learn about the world than do those who are sighted ..." (p. 394). Describe at least five implications of this statement for the education of young children who are blind.

3. "... the prevailing opinion ... that people with visual impairment were at risk to exhibit personality disturbances" (p. 400). In your opinion what accounts for this stereotype, and to what do the authors attribute the social difficulties which may arise for individuals with visual impairments?

4. "Most authorities agree that it is important to eliminate stereotypic behaviors" (p. 401). Do you support the effort to eliminate stereotypic behaviors in individuals who are blind? Why or why not?

5. "Many working-age adults with visual impairment are unemployed, and those who do work are often overqualified for the jobs they hold" (p. 417). Are you surprised by this statement? To what do the authors attribute this outcome?

III. Define the Terms

Write a definition for each of the following terms.

1. legally blind (p. 388)

2. Braille (pp. 388, 401-405)

3. low vision (p. 388)

4. The Snellen chart (pp. 389-390)

5. visual efficiency (p. 390)

6. myopia (p. 390)

7. hyperopia (pp. 390-391)

8. astigmatism (p. 390)

9. glaucoma (p. 391)

10. cataracts (p. 391)

11. diabetic retinopathy (p. 391)

12. retinitis pigmentosa (p. 392)

13. strabismus (p. 392)

14. nystagmus (p. 393)

15. mobility skills (pp. 394-396)

16. cognitive mapping (p. 395)

17. obstacle sense (p. 396)

18. Doppler effect (p. 396)

19. stereotypic behaviors (pp. 400-401)

20. blindisms (p. 401)

21. The Kurzweil Omni 1000 (p. 411)

22. BrailleMate (p. 411)

IV. Know the Content in This Chapter

A. Matching

a) Doppler effect
b) obstacle sense
c) blindisms
d) itinerant teacher services
e) mobility skills
f) stereotypic behaviors
g) cognitive mapping

1. _____ are very important for the successful adjustment of individuals with visual impairment--these skills depend to a great extent on spatial ability (pp. 394-396).

2. _____ refers to a map depicting the general relation of various points in the environment (p. 395).

3. _____ is the ability to detect physical obstructions in the environment (p. 396).

4. _____ a physical principle that says the pitch of a sound rises as a person moves toward its source (p. 396).

5. _____ refer to stereotypic behaviors manifested by individuals with blindness (pp. 400-401).

6. _____ repetitive, stereotyped movements such as body rocking, poking, or rubbing the eyes, repetitive hand or finger movements, or grimacing (pp. 400-401).

7. _____ a special educator who visits several different schools to work with students with visual impairments and their general education classroom teachers (pp. 412-413).

B. True or False

1. Blindness is among the least prevalent of all disabilities (p. 386). T or F

2. Most people who are blind can actually see (p. 386). T or F

115

3. People who are blind automatically develop better acuity in other senses (p. 387). T or F

4. Legal blindness qualifies a person for certain legal benefits, such as tax advantages and money for special materials (p. 388). T or F

5. A small percentage of individuals who are legally blind have absolutely no vision (p. 388). T or F

6. Visual acuity is most often measured with the Snellen chart (pp. 389-390). T or F

7. The amount of oxygen given to premature infants can cause blindness (p. 392). T or F

8. Most cases of strabismus are correctable with eye exercise or surgery (p. 392). T or F

9. IQ tests containing visual items more accurately measure the intelligence of individuals who are blind than tests containing verbally based items (p. 393). T or F

10. Good tactual perception, like good visual perception, relies on being able to use a variety of strategies (p. 394). T or F

11. Children who are totally blind do not depend more on the tactual sense for concept development than those with low vision (p. 394). T or F

12. People who are blind do not have lowered thresholds of sensation in touch or hearing (p. 396). T or F

13. The low achievement of some students who are blind may be due to low expectations and lack of exposure to Braille (p. 396). T or F

14. Most authorities agree that it is important to eliminate stereotypic behaviors (p. 401). T or F

15. Good listening skills develop automatically in children who are blind (p. 407). T or F

16. The guide dog is a frequently recommended aid to individuals who are blind (p. 409). T or F

C. Fill in the Blank

1. Educators often refer to individuals as having _____ if they have a visual impairment and can read print, even if they need magnifying devices or large print books to do so (p. 388).

2. Most visual problems are the result of errors of _____ (p. 390).

3. The most common visual impairments of low vision are _____ and _____(p. 390).

4. The pitch of a sound rises as a person moves toward its source, this phenomenon is knows as _____(p. 396).

5. Electronic devices for sensing objects in the environment are still expensive and largely experimental: examples of these devices are _____ and _____ (p. 411).

6. _____ converts print with almost any typeface into synthesized speech (p. 411).

7. Most students with visual impairment are educated either in _____ or _____ (p. 412).

8. An area of particular importance in early intervention for children with visual disabilities is _____ (p. 413).

9. During the transition to adulthood _____ and _____ are two closely related areas of difficulty for some adolescents and young adults with visual impairments (p. 414).

D. Multiple Choice

1. Which estimate most closely represents the number of individuals who are legally blind and who are also totally blind? (p. 388).
   a)   5 percent   d)   15 percent
   b)   1 percent   e)   18 percent
   c)   10 percent

2. What proportion of children aged 6-17 years of age are classified as visually impaired? (p. 388).
   a)   5 percent
   b)   .1 percent
   c)   .05 percent
   d)   .5 percent
   e)   none of the above

3. What problem is presented because some school personnel use only the Snellen chart as a screening procedure? (pp. 389-390).
   a)   The Snellen chart measures visual efficiency only.
   b)   Today more children are identified with visual impairments.
   c)   The Snellen chart does not pick up all types of visual problems and teachers should be alert to other signs of visual impairment.
   d)   The Snellen chart cannot be used to determine visual competence.

4. The Snellen chart is lacking in usefulness for predicting the ability to read print. This instrument measures: (p. 390)
   a)   visual efficiency
   b)   visual acuity for distant and not near objects
   c)   mobility skills
   d)   both a and c

5. IQ tests for individuals with blindness focus on: (p. 393)
   a)   visual skills
   b)   verbal skills
   c)   spatial and tactual skills
   d)   verbal and visual skills
   e)   both b and c

6. Mobility skills vary greatly among people with visual impairment. A critical variable appears to be: (p. 395)
   a)   cognitive mapping
   b)   visual acuity
   c)   motivation
   d)   Braille skills
   e)   technological aids

7. The most prevalent stereotypic behaviors in individuals who are blind are: (p. 401)
   a)   body rocking and eye poking
   b)   repetitive hand and finger movements
   c)   grimacing and repetitive body movements
   d)   all of the above

8. Over the past several years the use of Braille has: (p. 402)
   a) increased   d) remained unchanged
   b) decreased   e) declined dramatically
   c) fluctuated

9. Which of these does not aid the mobility of people with visual impairment? (p. 407).
   a) the long cane   d) human guides
   b) guide dogs   e) electronic devices
   c) Braille

10. The Kurzweil Omni 1000 is a technological aid which: (p. 411)
    a) converts print into synthesized speech
    b) has word processing capabilities
    c) provides a reader with ultrasonic sounds
    d) converts print to tactile letters
    e) none of the above

E. Short Answer

1. What different purposes are served by the legal and the educational definitions of blindness? (p. 388).

2. What is the difference between the vision of individuals who are legally blind and those who are partially sighted? (p. 388).

3. Describe the basic physiological structures of the visual system and briefly explain their functions (pp. 388-389).

4. Describe the two major factors which determine how the child will explore his/her environment (pp. 394-395).

5. Explain the development of the misconception that people who are blind have an extra sense (p. 396).

6. In what ways might, "telephone skills" facilitate communication between people with and people without blindness? (p. 400).

7. In typical classrooms children who have little or no sight frequently require special modifications in four specific areas. Describe these four areas (pp. 401-412).

8. What explanation may account for the decreased use of Braille since the 1960s? (pp. 401-405).

9. What beliefs account for the resistance to having children with visual impairment use their sight in reading and some other activities? (pp. 405-406).

10. What beliefs are held by those who advocate "sight conservation" and "sight-saving"? (p. 406).

11. Describe the four most frequently used educational placements for students with visual impairments (pp. 412-413).

12. How do the authors explain that infants who have visual impairments are often late to crawl? (pp. 413-414).

V.   Enrichment Activities

1. Record your experience following each of the following activities. How did you feel? How did the activity go? What adaptations would facilitate future attempts at these activities?
    Activity #1:   Wear a blindfold to simulate blindness and spend at least one hour socializing with a friend.
    Activity #2:   While wearing a blindfold, walk around your own home.
    Activity #3:   Walk around a friend's home while wearing a blindfold and guided by your friend.
    Activity #4:   Have dinner with a friend while wearing a blindfold.

2.   As you observe your community, in what ways are the special needs of individuals with visual impairments being addressed? In what ways are accessibility issues being addressed? What services are available in grocery stores, libraries, transit systems, and other mainstream environments to facilitate accessibility for individuals with visual impairments?

3.   Having observed your local community, what special issues have emerged relative to addressing the special needs of individuals who are blind? Based on your observations, make a list of the issues which need to be addressed, so that accessibility for individuals who have visual impairments is maximized in your community.

4.   Talk with an individual who has a visual impairment and who has agreed to talk with you about his/her disability. Ask him/her to tell you about his/her memories of school. What individuals, teaching methods, and materials facilitated his/her learning? What obstacles were particularly challenging? How does this individual view his/her future?

Answer Key for Chapter Ten

Matching		True or False		Multiple Choice	
1.	e	1.	T	1.	e
2.	g	2.	T	2.	c
3.	b	3.	F	3.	c
4.	a	4.	T	4.	b
5.	c	5.	T	5.	e
6.	f	6.	T	6.	c
7.	d	7.	T	7.	a
		8.	T	8.	e
		9.	F	9.	c
		10.	T	10.	a
		11.	F		
		12.	T		
		13.	T		
		14.	T		
		15.	F		
		16.	F		

Chapter 11

Physical Disabilities

I. **Important Points to Remember**

* Children with physical disabilities are those whose physical limitations or health problems interfere with their school attendance or learning to the point that they require special staff, services, equipment, materials, and facilities.

* Some children who have primary physical disabilities also have visual, auditory, or other secondary disabilities.

* Children with traumatic brain injury are now eligible to receive special education services under IDEA.

* The most widely accepted classification system for physical disabilities specifies the limbs involved and the type of motor disability.

* More children die or are seriously injured in accidents each year than are killed by all childhood diseases combined.

* Public attitudes can have a profound influence on how children with physical disabilities experience life in their families, schools and communities.

* Appropriate handling and positioning of children with physical disabilities makes them more comfortable and receptive to learning.

II. **Reflection and Discussion**

1. "... the population of children and youths with physical disabilities is growing but the availability of health and social service programs is not" (p. 428). Discuss at least five implications of this statement.

2.	"The effects of TBI may range from very mild to profound and may be temporary or permanent" (p. 430). Write three implications of this statement for parents and teachers.

3.	"... CP is a developmental disability--a multidisabling condition far more complex than a motor disability alone" (p. 433). What other disabilities often accompany the motor disability commonly observed in individuals with cerebral palsy?

4.	"... general and special education teachers may expect to encounter children who have seizures" (p. 434). What are the implications of this statement for the professional preparation of teachers?

5.	"... children exposed before birth to drugs are amenable to modification" (pp. 438-439). What is the implication of this statement for parents and teachers?

6.	"It is debatable as to which conditions are appropriate for children who are dependent on ventilators or other medical technology to attend regular classrooms" (p. 439). Would you agree that the regular classroom is or is not an appropriate placement for students who use ventilators and other medical technologies? Defend your position with a supporting rationale.

7.	"Children who are already disabled physically, mentally, or emotionally are more at risk for abuse than are nondisabled children" (p. 440). Are you surprised by this statement? What in your view would contribute to the increased risk for abuse among children with disabilities?

8.	"For children with physical disabilities, however, transition is perhaps a more pervasive concern than it is for children with other disabilities" (p. 456). Do you accept that transition is a more critical time for students with physical disabilities than it is for those with any other disability? Why or why not?

III.   Define the Terms

Write a definition for each of the following terms.

1.   congenital anomalies (p. 428)

2.   traumatic brain injury (p. 429)

3.   cerebral palsy (p. 432)

4.   selective posterior rhizotomy (p. 432)

5.   choreoathetoid movements (p. 433)

6.   atonic muscles (p. 433)

7.   spina bifida (p. 436)

8.   catheterization (p. 436)

9.   Tourette's syndrome (p. 437)

10.   tics (p. 437)

11.   muscular dystrophy (p. 437)

12.   juvenile rheumatoid arthritis (p. 437)

13.   fetal alcohol syndrome (p. 438)

14.   acquired immune deficiency syndrome (p. 438)

15.   prosthesis (p. 443)

16.   orthosis (p. 443)

17.   adaptive devices (p. 443)

18.   early intervention (pp. 454-456)

19. contractures (p. 455)

20. supported employment (pp. 457-458)

IV. **Know the Content in This Chapter**

A. **Matching**

a) spina bifida
b) quadriplegia
c) diplegia
d) paraplegia
e) hemiplegia
f) tics
g) contractions
h) spastic muscles
i) athetosis
j) orthosis
k) hypotonic muscles
l) handling

1. _____ is a motor disability or paralysis which involves the legs to a greater extent than the arms (p. 432).

2. _____ is a motor disability or paralysis of one side of the body (p. 432).

3. _____ is a motor disability or paralysis resulting from the involvement of all four limbs (p. 432).

4. _____ is a motor disability or paralysis which involves only the legs (p. 432).

5. _____ is a congenital midline defect resulting from failure of the bony spinal column to close completely during fetal development (p. 436).

6. _____ are repetitive movements, often accompanied by vocalizations of a socially inappropriate nature (p. 437).

7.	_____ is a device that enhances the partial function of a part of a person's body (p. 443).

8.	_____ cause children with disabilities to have either flexed or extended muscles all the time (p. 455).

9.	_____ is a permanent shortening of muscles and connective tissue which results in further deformity and disability (p. 455).

10.	_____ causes fluctuating muscle tone which results in almost constant uncontrolled movement (p. 455).

11.	_____ cause children to appear floppy, flaccid, and weak. They may also have difficulty holding their heads up, sitting, and standing (p. 455).

12.	_____ refers to how the child is picked up, carried, held, and assisted (p. 455).

**B.	True or False**

1.	Over 200,000 students with physical disabilities receive special education services (p. 428). T or F

2.	Children with traumatic brain injury may be eligible for special education and related services (p. 429). T or F

3.	Brain injuries can be caused by hypoxia, infection of the brain or its linings, tumors, metabolic disorders, or toxic chemicals (p. 429). T or F

4.	Females are more prone to traumatic brain injury than males (p. 429). T or F

5.	Cerebral palsy is a disease which is contagious and progressive (p. 432). T or F

6.	Some individuals have a mixture of various types of cerebral palsy (p. 433). T or F

7. Spina bifida is one of the most common birth defects resulting in physical disability; its causes are not known (p. 436). T or F

8. Juvenile rheumatoid arthritis involves the muscles and joints and it is sometimes accompanied by complications such as fever, respiratory problems, heart problems and eye infections (p. 437). T or F

9. The intelligence of children with muscular dystrophy and arthritis is usually seriously and negatively affected (p. 437). T or F

10. More children die in accidents each year than are killed by all childhood diseases combined (p. 438). T or F

11. Children with AIDS often acquire neurological problems including mental retardation, cerebral palsy, or behavioral disorders (p. 438). T or F

12. Teenage mothers are more likely than older women to give birth to premature babies who are at high risk for a variety of physical disabilities and psychological disorders (p. 439). T or F

13. Children with disabilities, including those with physical disabilities, are at a more increased risk for abuse than nondisabled children (p. 440). T or F

14. Children with physical disabilities versus those with neurological impairments are more likely to lag behind their peers in academic achievement (p. 441). T or F

15. Though an individual with severe spastic quadriplegia may have a bright mind, he/she must accept that only a very limited number of potential occupations are available to him/her (p. 457). T or F

16. Severe physical disabilities kill sexual desire, prevent sexual gratification and preclude marriage and children (p. 459). T or F

C. Fill in the Blank

1. _____ involves a penetrating head wound which may be caused by a fall, a gunshot wound, a vehicular accident, or surgery (p. 429).

2. A _____ damages the brain and is caused by internal compression, stretching, or other shearing motion of neural tissue within the head (p. 429).

3. Stiffness or tenseness of muscles and inaccurate voluntary movement is known as _____ (p. 433).

4. A person has a _____ when there is an abnormal discharge of electrical energy in specific brain cells (p. 433).

5. _____ results when the spinal column fails to close completely during fetal development (p. 436).

6. _____ are sudden repetitive movements which are often accompanied by socially inappropriate vocalizations (p. 437).

7. _____ is a painful and potentially debilitating disease in which affects the muscles and joints of children (p. 437).

8. A teacher who fails to report child abuse or neglect may be held legally _____ (p. 440).

9. A missing body part is replaced by a _____ (p. 443).

10. The partial functioning of a body part is enhanced with a _____ (p. 443).

D. Multiple Choice

1. Which number most closely represents the statistics from the U.S. Department of Education on how many students with physical disabilities receive special education services? (p. 428).
   a)   100,000   c)   250,000
   b)   150,000   d)   200,000

2. What is the estimated percentage of school-age children who acquire a brain injury each year? (p. 429).
    a) .5 percent   c) 2 percent
    b) .10 percent   d) .3 percent

3. What is the estimated percentage of students who have traumatic brain injury by the time they graduate from high school: (p. 429)
    a) 1 percent   d) 4 percent
    b) 1.5 percent   e) 2 percent
    c) 3 percent

4. Which of the following symptoms are almost always present when a child's nervous system is damaged? (p. 431).
    a) high levels of frustration, fatigue and irritability
    b) poor social and behavioral skills
    c) muscular weakness or paralysis
    d) long- and short-term memory loss
    e) cognitive and social/behavioral deficits

5. One of the most common types of cerebral palsy involves either the right or left side of the body: (p. 432)
    a) hemiplegia   d) paraplegia
    b) diplegia   e) choreoathetoid
    c) quadriplegia

6. This is a rare neurological disorder that typically affects a child's ability to communicate, form social relationships, and perform normally on tests of intelligence and academic achievement: (p. 436)
    a) Asperger syndrome   d) spina bifida
    b) Tourette's syndrome   e) fetal alcohol syndrome
    c) autism

7. Which of the following is the leading cause of injury - both physical and psychological - and death among children? (p. 440).
    a) accidents   d) AIDS
    b) abuse and neglect   e) none of the above
    c) poor prenatal care

8. Children under the age of three years who need special education and related services are required by law to have: (p. 448)

8. Children under the age of three years who need special education and related services are required by law to have: (p. 448)
   a) an individualized education plan
   b) an individualized family service plan
   c) a transition plan
   d) an annual medical examination
   e) a preschool assessment battery

9. All who work with young children with physical disabilities have two concerns. These are: (p. 454)
   a) physical and social development
   b) family involvement in education
   c) early identification and intervention
   d) development of communication skills
   e) c and d only

10. Two areas of concern for transition stand out clearly for adolescents and adults with physical disabilities. These are: (p. 456)
   a) employment and continued education
   b) health insurance coverage and housing
   c) careers and sociosexuality
   d) higher education and social integration
   e) access to the workplace and work skills

E. Short Answer

1. When does the child's physical condition become the concern not just of the medical profession but of teaching specialists as well? (pp. 426, 428).

2. What risk factors in the environment place individuals at increased risk for physical disabilities? (p. 328).

3. What is the difference between open and closed head injuries? (p. 429).

4. Define traumatic brain injury using the four specifications outlined in the text (pp. 429-431).

5. What causes have been attributed to the development of cerebral palsy? (pp. 432-433).

6. What are the most common causes of seizures? (pp. 433-436).

7. Name at least five unhealthy practices which cause disabilities and which could be avoided (pp. 439-441).

8. What public attitudes facilitate overall positive life experiences for children with physical disabilities? (p. 442).

9. What guidance do the authors provide for the selection of the most useful prosthetics, orthosis, or adaptive devices? (pp. 443, 445-447).

10. Why is it so important that teachers should know the medical histories of their students who have physical disabilities? (pp. 450-451, 454).

11. Describe the two primary concerns of educators in early intervention programs for young children with physical disabilities? (pp. 454-456).

12. What primary provisions does the Americans with Disabilities Act make for adults with disabilities? (p. 457).

V.   Enrichment Activities

1.   In the film *My Left Foot* (1989), Daniel Day-Lewis plays the role of a young man with cerebral palsy. Evaluate the portrayal of an individual with a physical disability in this film. Is this a realistic portrayal? Does the hero seem credible to you? What aspect(s) of this film did you like most? What aspects did you like least?

2.   Read *Under The Eye of the Clock: The Life Story of Christopher Nolan*, C. Nolan (St. Martin's Press, 1987). Consider the contribution of this book. In what way(s) does this story help a reader to understand the lives of individuals with disabilities? Would you recommend this book to a friend? Why or why not?

3.   Use a wheelchair or any other prosthetic device for at least three to four hours while conducting your daily routine. Following this experience, describe your interactions with others. In what way(s) was your experience of life different and/or not so different while using the prosthetic device? What did you learn through your simulation of a physical disability?

Answer Key for Chapter Eleven

Matching		True or False		Multiple Choice	
1.	c	1.	T	1.	d
2.	e	2.	T	2.	a
3.	b	3.	T	3.	d
4.	d	4.	F	4.	c
5.	a	5.	F	5.	a
6.	f	6.	T	6.	c
7.	j	7.	T	7.	b
8.	h	8.	T	8.	b
9.	g	9.	F	9.	e
10.	i	10.	T	10.	c
11.	k	11.	T		
12.	l	12.	T		
		13.	T		
		14.	F		
		15.	F		
		16.	F		

Chapter 12

Special Gifts and Talents

I.   **Important Points to Remember**

*   There is no professionally agreed upon definition of giftedness.

*   Though giftedness has been recognized throughout history, today some individuals who are gifted remain unrecognized.

*   In the United States, individuals who are gifted often experience social stigma and rejection.

*   Children with special gifts excel in some area(s) compared to other children of the same age.

*   Giftedness is not a disability in the usual sense and it is not a defined special education category in IDEA.

*   Researchers propose that individuals who are gifted demonstrate high ability, high creativity, and high task commitment.

*   Genetics and environmental factors, among others, influence the development of superior abilities.

*   Individually administered intelligence tests alone are not sufficient to determine superior abilities.

*   The use of multiple criteria in the identification of children who are gifted helps to avoid bias toward traditionally neglected groups.

*   Some children who are gifted are underachievers, have disabilities, and cross all cultural and social boundaries.

*   Females are the largest single group of neglected gifted students.

* Giftedness is dynamic rather than static and it may be present or not present at different times in an individual's life.

* Students who are gifted may require extraordinary adaptations in the school setting.

* A variety of educational programs are used to address the unique educational needs of students who are gifted.

* Teachers of students who are gifted should be particularly committed to excellence in teaching and student learning.

* Acceleration and enrichment are important considerations in programs for adolescents who are gifted.

* Educational programs for young children who are gifted address their advanced skills and their social and emotional development.

II. Reflection and Discussion

1. "... we may wonder about our moral obligation to help someone who is already advantaged become even better ..." (p. 468). Do you believe that students with gifts have special educational needs? Why or why not?

2. "Giftedness is invented, not discovered" (p. 471). What do the authors mean by this statement?

3. "... we should speak of people who exhibit gifted *behavior*, rather than of gifted *people* ..." (p. 475). Do you agree that gifts in people are observable only in certain circumstances? Or, do you believe that gifts are inherent in individuals? Use an example to illustrate your answer.

4. "But not all such [gifted] students enjoy occupational success in demanding jobs; some choose career paths that do not make use of their talents or otherwise fail to distinguish themselves ..." (p. 480). Does this statement surprise you? How would you explain why individuals with superior abilities may not be successful in their personal and/or professional lives?

5.   "Special programs for students with special gifts and talents remain highly controversial" (p. 484). Are you surprised by this statement? Do you support special educational programming for students who are gifted? State at least three reasons to support your position.

6.   "Many females achieve far less than they might because of social or cultural barriers to their selection or progress in certain careers" (p. 486). Do you agree with this statement? Why or why not?

7.   "... giftedness is in the performance, not the person" (p. 487). Do you agree with this statement? Why or why not? Support your answer with at least one example.

8.   "In fact, giftedness can occur in combination with disabilities of nearly every description ..." (p. 489). What special challenges are offered to teachers of students who are gifted and who have disabilities?

III.   Define the Terms

Write a definition for each of the following terms.

1.   precocity (p. 471)

2.   insight (p. 471)

3.   genius (p. 471)

4.   creativity (p. 471)

5.   giftedness (p. 471)

6.   talent (p. 471)

7.   analytic giftedness (p. 473)

8.   synthetic giftedness (p. 474)

9.   practical giftedness (p. 474)

10.   enrichment (p. 493)

11. acceleration (p. 493)

12. schoolwide enrichment model (p. 496)

IV. Know the Content in This Chapter

A. Matching

a) analytic giftedness
b) synthetic giftedness
c) practical giftedness
d) precocity
e) insight
f) genius
g) creativity
h) giftedness
i) talent
j) enrichment
k) acceleration
l) schoolwide enrichment model

1. _____ remarkable early development in particular areas such as language, music, or math (p. 471).

2. _____ cognitive superiority, creativity, and motivation such that an individual is set apart from peers and is able to contribute to society in a highly valued manner (p. 471).

3. _____ is a special ability or aptitude (p. 471).

4. _____ is extremely rare intellectual power (p. 471).

5. _____ the ability to separate relevant from irrelevant information or finding new and novel ways of combining new and old information (p. 471).

6. _____ is the ability to express novel and useful ideas or to ask previously unthought of but useful questions (p. 471).

7.   _____ being able to take a problem apart, understand the parts of a problem, and how these parts are interrelated (p. 473).

8.   _____ insight, creativity, intuition, or adeptness at coping with novel situations. This is characteristic of people who choose careers in the arts and sciences (p. 474).

9.   _____ applying analytic and synthetic abilities to problem-solving. This is characteristic of people who have successful careers (p. 474).

10. _____ is the practice of placing students in educational programs designed for students who are ahead of their same age-mates (p. 493).

11. _____ additional experiences provided to students without placing them in a higher grade (p. 493).

12. _____ was designed to address the need to reduce the separateness of special and regular programs and to make certain that all students who can benefit from enrichment activities are given the opportunity to participate in them (p. 496).

B.   True or False

1.   Professionals have a clear and agreed-on definition of giftedness (pp. 468, 470-471). T or F

2.   Federal law requires that students who are gifted have a right to receive a special education (p. 471). T or F

3.   Professionals agree that individually administered standard intelligence tests are the most reliable tests to measure intelligence (p. 471). T or F

4.   Most children who are gifted learn to read easily and before entering school (p. 480). T or F

5.   Unhappiness, emotional instability, and social rejection characterizes the lives of many individuals who are gifted (p. 480). T or F

6. Extraordinary adaptations of schooling are seldom required for students who are gifted (p. 481). T or F

7. Cooperative learning and peer tutoring are excellent strategies for the education of students who are truly gifted (p. 485). T or F

8. Acceleration is typically sufficient to address the problems of the underachieving gifted student (p. 487). T or F

9. Giftedness resides in the person rather than in the performance (p. 487). T or F

10. Experts agree that accelerated programs are clearly more desirable than enrichment programs (pp. 492-496). T or F

11. There is little evidence of support for early intervention programs for young children who are gifted (p. 500). T or F

12. Transitions for youths who are gifted tend to mirror the problem in transitions faced by adolescents and young adults with disabilities (p. 502). T or F

C.   Fill in the Blank

1. An extraordinary ability to understand the parts of a problem and how these parts are interrelated in known as _____ giftedness (p. 473).

2. _____ giftedness involves insight, intuition, creativity, or adeptness at coping with novel situations (p. 474).

3. An extraordinary capacity to apply analytic and synthetic abilities to the solution of everyday problems is known as _____ (p. 474).

4. _____ refers to superior abilities in specific areas of performance, which may be exhibited under some circumstances but not under others (p. 475).

5. Malnutrition or neurological damage can _____ giftedness from developing (p. 477).

6. _____ comprise the largest group of neglected gifted students (p. 490).

7. Programs which provide students with additional learning experiences while they remain in the grade levels appropriate for their chronological age are known as _____ programs (p. 493).

8. In _____ programs, students who are gifted are placed in grade levels which are ahead of their peers in one or more subject areas (p. 493).

9. The _____ model is based on the notion that children exhibit gifted behaviors in relation to particular projects or activities to which they apply their above-average ability, creativity, and task commitment (p. 496).

10. Talented adolescents are _____ first and foremost (p. 503).

D. Multiple Choice

1. At which level is educational policy on gifted education programming most influential? (p. 471).
    a) federal
    b) state
    c) local
    d) regional
    e) school district

2. Why are individual intelligence tests insufficient for defining giftedness? (pp. 471-475).
    a) Above average intellectual functioning is not essential in order to be identified as gifted.
    b) IQ tests do not reliably or validly assess insight and creativity.
    c) IQ tests are not valid or reliable assessment instruments.
    d) Deductive thinking is not assessed in IQ tests.

3.	What three kinds of giftedness did Sternberg propose? (pp. 473-474).
	a)	conceptual, social, and analytical
	b)	creativity, insight, and precocity
	c)	analytic, synthetic, and practical
	d)	artistic and scientific
	e)	none of the above

4.	Some professionals propose that the criteria for judging whether someone is gifted involves: (p. 475)
	a)	excellence in one or more dimensions of performance
	b)	rarity and value - meaning that few peers exhibit such characteristic(s) and this is highly valued by society
	c)	demonstrability - actually exhibiting a rare ability through some type of valid assessment
	d)	productivity - the person is actually producing something
	e)	all of the above

5.	According to federal reports and legislation, what percentage of the school-age children may be considered gifted? (p. 475).
	a)	.5 percent		d)	2 percent
	b)	1 percent		e)	3-5 percent
	c)	1.5 percent

6.	What factors determine a child's intelligence? (p. 476).
	a)	environmental		d)	nutritional
	b)	genetic and biological		e)	all of the above
	c)	social and cultural

7.	What characteristics may be observed in gifted students who have unique needs because of their cultural or minority status? (pp. 486-487).
	a)	cultural diversity
	d)	socioeconomic deprivation
	c)	geographic isolation
	d)	all of the above

8.   The largest group of neglected students who are gifted is: (p. 490)
      a)   children under the age of five
      b)   youths over the age of fifteen
      c)   females
      d)   children with disabilities
      e)   none of the above

9.   Programs which involve placing children who are gifted in grades
      which are higher than their same-age peers are called: (p. 493)
      a)   schoolwide enrichment programs
      b)   acceleration programs
      c)   enrichment programs
      d)   independent study programs
      e)   advanced class placement programs

10.   Programs which are designed to permit students to remain in them
      as long as they have the ability, creativity, and motivation to pursue
      productive activities that go beyond the usual curriculum for
      students their age are called: (p. 496)
      a)   enrichment programs
      b)   acceleration programs
      c)   pull-out programs
      d)   consultant teacher programs
      e)   schoolwide enrichment programs

11.   Which of the following statements is true: Teaching students who
      are gifted is: (pp. 497)
      a)   the easiest teaching assignment because the students learn
            so quickly and so easily
      b)   the most challenging group of students with which a teacher
            will ever work
      c)   best done by teachers who foster students' creativity, have
            developed their own creative competencies, and are able to
            use creative teaching procedures with great skill
      d)   the most rewarding professional assignment for teachers
            who are eager to learn

12. Which one of the following statements about transitions for adolescents who are gifted is true? (p. 502).
    a) Transitions are more problematic for them than for any other group of students.
    b) Adolescents who are gifted tend to mirror the problems in transitions faced by adolescents with disabilities.
    c) Because of their high intelligence, transitions do not impact the lives of these students.
    d) None of the above are true.

E. **Short Answer**

1. How would you characterize the way children who are gifted are regarded in U.S. culture and educational policy? (pp. 468, 470-471).

2. In what areas do professionals pose questions about the definition of giftedness? (p. 470).

3. Besides the word "gifted," what word(s) would you prefer to use to describe individuals who have superior ability in some area(s)? (pp. 470-471).

4. What are the common elements in the definitions of giftedness which are used in several states? (p. 471).

5. Why is ability grouping one of the most controversial topics related to school reform? (p. 485).

6. Which features of classrooms are highly motivating to students? (p. 487).

7. What do the authors suggest to increase the number of students from diverse backgrounds in gifted programs? (pp. 487-489).

8.   What do the authors recommend when teachers and schools are unable to provide the extensive services that students who are gifted often need? (pp. 487-489).

9.   What steps did the authors propose in order to increase the number of females who receive education and choose careers which are commensurate with their abilities? (pp. 490, 492).

10.   Describe the schoolwide enrichment model, proposed by Renzulli and his colleagues, for the education of students who are gifted (p. 496).

11.   Describe the unique professional challenges and responsibilities which await teachers of students who are gifted (p. 497).

12.   Do you support the development of early intervention programs for young children who are gifted? Why or why not? (p. 497, 500-502).

V.   Enrichment Activities

1.   Let us imagine that along with the twenty students assigned to your classroom are Sarah, John, and Ramon. Sarah is ten years old, identified as gifted and she has a communication disorder. John is almost eleven years old, identified as gifted and he has a learning disability, and Ramon is nine and a half, identified as gifted and he has a learning disability. In the past, these students have challenged their teachers in unique ways. List at least ten challenges you would expect as a teacher of these students.

2.   Visit with a principal of a local public school and find out what educational programming is available for students who are gifted. Following your visit, consider to what extent you believe that this represents adequate educational programming. Describe the strong points of this program and consider what you would recommend to enhance or further strengthen this program.

3.   Read *Girl Interrupted* by S. Kaysen (Vintage Books/Random House, 1994). In what ways was Susanna Kaysen interrupted? Did reading this book influence your thinking about adolescents who are gifted and particularly, girls who are gifted? What in your opinion is the most valuable contribution of this book?

Answer Key for Chapter Twelve

Matching		True or False		Multiple Choice	
1.	d	1.	F	1.	b
2.	h	2.	F	2.	b
3.	i	3.	F	3.	c
4.	f	4.	T	4.	e
5.	e	5.	F	5.	e
6.	g	6.	F	6.	e
7.	a	7.	F	7.	d
8.	b	8.	F	8.	c
9.	c	9.	F	9.	b
10.	k	10.	F	10.	e
11.	j	11.	T	11.	c
12.	l	12.	T	12.	b

Chapter 13

Parents and Families

I.   **Important Points to Remember**

*   Parents affect children's behavior and children affect parents' behavior.

*   Though it is true that parents of children go through a series of stages after learning that they have a child with a disability, it is important that we do not expect them to go through these stages in a lockstep manner.

*   Everyday routines that most families take for granted are frequently disrupted in families with a child with a disability.

*   Some parents report that adding a child with a disability to the family actually has some unanticipated positive results.

*   Few data are available on the reaction of siblings to their brothers and sisters with disabilities.

*   Professionals today are more likely to recognize the positive influence of parents on the development of children with disabilities.

*   During the last twenty years demographic changes and more stressful living conditions have reduced the amount of parental support that is available for children with disabilities.

*   When parents talk with their children about disabilities, they must take precautions not to alarm or underestimate the impact of a disability.

*   Talking with children about their disabilities is best done before their teenage years.

* The response of families to children with disabilities is largely determined by their family characteristics, family interaction, family functions, and family life cycle.

* Informal sources of support, such as extended family, friends, church groups, neighbors, and social clubs help families cope with the stress of having a child with a disability.

II. Reflection and Discussion

1. "A fertile ground for conflict or harmony, the family-- especially the family with a member who has a disability--is the perfect locale for studying the interplay of human emotion and behavior" (p. 514). In what ways might families with a member who has a disability be more challenged than families without a member who has a disability?

2. "They [professionals] now recognize that the family of the person with a disability, especially the parents, can help in their educational efforts" (p. 514). Do you agree that the families of persons with disabilities are important in the education of students with disabilities? Support you arguments with specific examples.

3. "Sometimes the parent changes the behavior of the child or infant; sometimes the reverse is true" (p. 516). What are the implications of this statement?

4. "The birth of any child can have a significant effect on the dynamics of the family ... the effects on the family of the birth of a child who has a disability can be even more profound" (p. 517). In what ways do you expect that the birth of a child with a disability would have profound effects on a family? Provide examples to illustrate your conclusions.

5. "Although a relatively large body of literature pertains to parental reactions, there is much less information about siblings of persons with disabilities" (p. 522). Do you expect that the reactions of siblings would be the same as or different from the reactions of parents of children with disabilities? In what ways?

6. "... many families of students with disabilities prefer a passive, rather than an active, degree of involvement in their children's education" (p. 529). Are you surprised by this? Why or why not?

7. "Transitions between stages in the life cycle are particularly stressful for families, especially families with children who are disabled" (p. 529). Provide examples of particular difficulties with transitions from early childhood to school-age to adolescence and later to adulthood which families of children with disabilities may experience.

8. "...we are just beginning to harness the expertise of families so we can provide the best possible programs for their children" (p. 538). Do you agree or disagree with this statement? Support your beliefs with specific examples.

III. Define the Terms

Write a definition for each of the following terms.

1. the eugenics movement (p. 514)

2. PL 105-17 (p. 516)

3. Individualized Family Service Plan (p. 516)

4. Family centered models (pp. 524-526)

5. Family cohesion (pp. 527-528)

6. Family adaptability (pp. 528-529)

7. Family functions (p. 529)

8. Family life cycle (pp. 529-530)

9. Home-note programs (p. 535)

10. Advocacy (p. 536)

IV. Know the Content in This Chapter

A. Matching

    a)   PL 105-17
    b)   family functions
    c)   Individualized Family Service Plan
    d)   adaptability of families
    e)   cohesion among family members

1. ____is mandated by PL 105-17 which requires that schools must involve parents in the education of their young children with disabilities (p. 516).

2. ____ stipulates that school professionals make a concerted effort to involve parents and families in the education of their children with disabilities (p. 516).

3. ____ refers to the degree to which an individual family member is free to act independently of other family members (pp. 527-528).

4. ____ refers to the degree to which families are able to change their modes of interaction when they encounter unusual or stressful situations (p. 528).

5. ____ the numerous tasks and activities in which families engage to meet their many and diverse needs (p. 529).

B. True or False

1. Mothers are primarily responsible for the development of autism (p. 514). T or F

2. Parents need training before they can become involved with the professionals who work their children (p. 516). T or F

3. IDEA and PL 105-17 stipulate that school personnel must make a concerted effort to involve parents and families in educational programming for their children with disabilities (p. 516). T or F

4. Everyday routines that most families take for granted are frequently disrupted in families with children who are disabled (p. 517). T or F

5. Evidence is abundant that parents of children with disabilities undergo more than the average amount of stress (p. 520). T or F

6. The majority of parents of children with disabilities have major psychological problems (p. 521). T or F

7. Teachers can sometimes play an important role in helping students to adjust to their siblings with disabilities (p. 524). T or F

8. Professionals today are more likely to recognize the positive influences parents can have on the development of their children with disabilities (p. 524-526). T or F

9. The family systems approach is built on the assumption that it is better to enable families to help themselves than to provide only direct services to them (p. 526). T or F

10. Cohesion and adaptability make no difference to the health of a family (pp. 527-529). T or F

11. Parents can consider giving household chores to their children who have disabilities (p. 528). T or F

12. Researchers have found that many families of students with disabilities prefer a passive rather than an active degree of involvement in their children's education (p. 529). T or F

13. Social support refers to formal supports designed to provide social, emotional and educational programming to young children with disabilities (p. 530). T or F

14. In traveling notebooks teachers and other professionals, such as speech and physical therapists, can write brief messages to parents and vice versa (p. 536). T or F

C. Fill in the Blank

1. The focus of _____ is not only on the child with a disability but also on his/her family. It describes the services the family needs to enhance the child's development (p. 516).

2. Researchers and clinicians have suggested that parents go through a series of _____ after finding out that they have a child with a disability (p. 517).

3. Based on the Stage Theory Approach, the final stage parents go through is _____ (p. 517).

4. There is no universal _____ reaction to the added stress of raising a child with a disability (p. 521).

5. Family size, cultural background, socioeconomic level are family _____ (p. 526).

6. The degree to which a member of the family is free to act independently of other family members is known as _____ (p. 527).

7. The degree to which families are able to change their modes of interaction when they encounter new or stressful situations is known as _____ (p. 528).

8. A component of the Turnbulls' family systems model which includes daily care, social needs, and medical and educational needs is known as family _____ (p. 529).

9. _____ means that one person has the authority, granted by the courts, to make decisions for another person (p. 529).

10. _____ can be an effective way for teachers and parents to share information (p. 534).

11. When teachers have a way of communicating with parents and having them reinforce the behavior that occurs in school they are using _____ (p. 535).

12. A system of communication in which parents and professionals write messages to each other by way of a notebook or log that accompanies the child to and from school is called _____(p. 536).

D. Multiple Choice

1. In the late 1970s and early 1980s professionals became less likely to blame parents for the problems encountered by their children. Why? (pp. 514, 516)
    a) Parents are not the cause of their children's problems.
    b) Causes of children's problems are usually reciprocal.
    c) Solutions for children's problems can often be found by enlisting the assistance of families.
    d) both b and c

2. An Individualized Family Service Plan focuses on the: (p. 516)
    a) child
    b) community
    c) child and family
    d) family
    e) family and the community

3. Which of the following best characterizes the response of parents to their children with disabilities? (p. 521).
    a) Parents of children with mild disabilities undergo more stress than the parents of children without disabilities.
    b) Parents learn from their children with disabilities.
    c) There is no universal parental reaction to the added stress of raising a child with a disability.
    d) None of the above are true.

4. Which one of the following statements best characterizes the adjustments of parents and siblings to children with disabilities? (p. 521).
    a) Most parents and siblings without disabilities adapt poorly to children with disabilities.
    b) The adjustment of parents and siblings is directly related to their socioeconomic status and educational level.
    c) Some parents and siblings have trouble adjusting, some have no trouble adjusting, and some actually appear to benefit from the experience.
    d) None of the above are true.

5. Which response of children to their siblings with disabilities is most accurate? (p. 522).
    a) Children who have siblings with disabilities are often unaware of the unique needs of their siblings until they reach adolescence.
    b) Children who have siblings with disabilities frequently experience the same emotions--fear, anger, guilt, and so forth—that their parents do.
    c) Nondisabled children frequently blame their parents for the disabilities of their siblings.
    d) Children who have siblings with disabilities are warm, accepting, and welcoming of their siblings and of all others with disabilities.
    e) None of the above are true.

6. Under which of the following circumstances do children have a particularly difficult challenge adjusting to their siblings with disabilities? (pp. 522-524).
    a) when siblings are close together in age
    b) same gender siblings with disabilities
    c) older girls who have a younger sibling with a disability
    d) all of the above

7. Which of the following is *not* a component of Turnbulls' Family Systems Approach? (p. 526).
    a) family support systems
    b) the characteristics of families
    c) family life cycles
    d) the interactions among family members
    e) family functions

8. Family systems theorists believe that: (p. 526)
    a) professionals' roles are defined relative to family needs
    b) families must unite and form a unique system before they seek the assistance of professionals
    c) social systems are relevant only to the extent that they address family relationships
    d) all parts of the family are interrelated; events affecting any one family member also have an effect on the others

9. "Mary has a severe hearing impairment and is developmentally delayed. She is being raised by a single mother along with three younger siblings. This family lives in a small city ..." According to the Turnbulls' Family Systems Approach, of which component is this statement reflective? (p. 526).

a   family functions   d) family interactions
b) family characteristics   e) none of the above
c) family life cycles

10. Transitions in the life of a child with a disability are particularly difficult because: (p. 530)

a) parents are not ready to permit their child with a disability to be independent
b) additional professionals become involved in their lives and this creates new stressors
c) new challenges are overwhelming to families of a child with a disability
d) transitions bring new uncertainties into the family
e) b and d only

11. The most important component of an effective and productive parent-teacher partnership is: (p. 532)

a) friendship   d) creative decision-making
b) trust   e) communication
c) honesty

12. Most authorities agree that parent and teacher cooperation is most readily established through the use of: (p. 533)

a) the Internet   d) success stories
b) parent support groups e) communication devices,
c) homework   i.e., home-notes, etc.

E. Short Answer

1. Do you agree with the observation that the addition of a child with a disability to a family could have unanticipated positive results? Defend your conclusion and support it with at least three credible examples (pp. 520-521).

2.   Describe different situations which tend to cause siblings of children with disabilities to develop negative attitudes (pp. 523-524).

3.   What major change is reflected in the use of family-centered models? (pp. 524-526).

4.   What four interrelated components are addressed in the family systems approach? (p. 526).

5.   In what ways might family characteristics have implications for intervention programming? (pp. 526-527).

6.   In what ways have family characteristics changed over the last 20 years? Why are these characteristics relevant to family-centered programming? (pp. 526-527).

7.   What is the major difference in the focus of the family systems approach and the social support systems approach? (pp. 526-532).

8.   Do you accept the conclusion that families are healthier if they have moderate degrees of cohesion and adaptability? Defend your conclusions using specific examples (pp. 527-528).

9.   What is the impact of high and low cohesion among family members? (pp. 527-528).

10. What particular dangers may an individual with a disability be exposed to in a family characterized by low adaptability? (p. 528).

11. What explanation do Hallahan and Kauffman offer for why parents may *not* wish to be highly involved in the development of their child's IEP? (p. 529).

12. In what ways are parent support groups helpful to families of children with disabilities? (pp. 530-531).

V. Enrichment Activities

1. While assuring confidentiality and willingness of the family to provide information, talk with a family of a child with a disability at the elementary or high school level. Discuss the impact of this child on the family. Ask the parents/guardians to identify their strongest allies and their greatest liabilities in the growth and development of their child and family.

2. Read *Deaf Like Me* by T. S. Spradley and J. P. Spradley (Gallaudet University, 1985). How do the authors portray Lynn's parents? Is this a realistic portrayal? What new insight(s) do you have into the lives of parents of children with disabilities after reading this book?

Answer Key for Chapter Thirteen

Matching		True or False		Multiple Choice	
1.	a	1.	F	1.	d
2.	c	2.	F	2.	c
3.	e	3.	T	3.	c
4.	d	4.	T	4.	c
5.	b	5.	T	5.	b
		6.	F	6.	d
		7.	T	7.	a
		8.	T	8.	d
		9.	F	9.	b
		10.	F	10.	e
		11.	T	11.	e
		12.	T	12.	e
		13.	F		
		14.	T		

NOTES

NOTES

NOTES

NOTES

NOTES

NOTES

NOTES

NOTES

NOTES